# THE BUSINESS YOU CAN START

## SPOTTING THE GREATEST OPPORTUNITIES IN THE ECONOMIC DOWNTURN

By Victor Kwegyir

Published by VicCor Wealth Publishing

ISBN: 0956770614
ISBN-13: 9780956770615

To contact Victor for speaking engagements please send an email to thebizucanstart@gmail.com. For the best deals for bulk orders please contact viccorwealthpublishers@gmail.com. Thank you for your business.

# DEDICATION

I dedicate this book to Coretta, my beautiful Wife who has stood with me through the thick and thin since our marriage; to my Mum, who has sacrificed so much for me over the years; and above all to God and Jesus Christ my LORD and personal saviour, who awakened in me the much needed passion and ability to write this book.

# ACKNOWLEDGEMENT

Writing a book doesn't happen without help, especially for a first book such as this. I will like to thank all those who helped make it possible.

Thank you CreateSpace Publishing, for the professional comprehensive editorial and design services in bringing this book to the highest professional quality.

Thank you Michael Ajose, a Technical Analyst at London Stock Exchange, for being a constant and reliable friend and for all your suggestions and remarks. Your help and friendship has been invaluable.

Thank you Mr & Mrs Babtunde of Dominion Glow Ltd, leaders of my House Fellowship, and the rest of the members of the fellowship, for your prayers and support.

Thank you Effie Smillie, founder and CEO of Rainbow Medical Services Ltd, for being such an inspiring and supportive business friend.

Thank you Sam & Vero Acquaye, Executive Director of Finance Merchant Bank Ltd, for your immense faith in me and support over the years.

Thank you Coretta, Mum and my four wonderful Sisters (Theodora, Natalia, Dorothy & Marian) for your love and prayers over the years.

Thank you, all my valuable clients for your business and enriching experience gained in working with you.

Thank you Pastor Mathew Ashimolowo, President and Senior Pastor of Kingsway International Christian Centre, for the challenging and inspiring teaching and programmes that infuse confidence and stirs up creativity in people like me.

Thank you God, who has made me all that I am and everything there is to be thankful for in life.

# INTRODUCTION

In the midst of the global economic crisis, some interesting stories are being written and rewritten. Ironically whilst corporations and governments face great uncertainties and are cutting back, there are almost daily announcements of new business start ups, corporate expansions and profits being made all around us, not to mention the growth in certain economies.

The question is, could these challenges be a source of blessing in disguise? This is what I believe, and exactly what the book is all about. Challenges have a way of spurring people into action. Interestingly every question in life needs answers, every problem needs solving and every challenge needs someone to face it head on and overcome it, and fortunately none of these will stop as long as life exists.

In any case, each individual, to a large extent, has a responsibility to at least survive in life.

The times may have inspired you to consider a career change or start of your own business. You might be looking for extra income, facing the threat of losing your job or have already lost your job. Conversely you may not have thought of any of the reasons stated here. Regardless of the category you fall into this is a book you *must* own!

"The Business You Can Start - Spotting The Greatest Opportunities In The Economic Downturn" challenges and inspires you to take a second look at the economy, anywhere in the world, and see the *Rare Business Opportunities* staring right in your face, that you can take full advantage of.

The facts and opportunities identified by this book will help you uncover the rare secrets that have transformed the lives of many and affirm the fact that times of economic difficulty are opportune times for those willing to apply the principles to succeed.

These people seized the opportunities and started great businesses many of which have become household names today.

Very importantly, this book also shows the reader *Thirty Smart Ways* of how to *Identify Business Opportunities* right where you are and further afield, anywhere on the planet. It further explains with clearly defined steps how to develop your ideas, dreams and skills into viable business ventures.

"The Business You Can Start" has *Proven Winning Strategies and Principles* that when applied can greatly help you to start a business, distinguish yourself from the competition and cause your enterprise to grow profitably and successfully.

This informative book also contains a *Comprehensive and Professional Practical Business Plan Guide*. It is structured and designed simply for the users' greatest flexibility. It can be adapted and used as a guide in writing a plan fit for any purpose and to meet the needs of any end user.

The marketplace richly rewards entrepreneurs for the problems they solve. Think of that and let this book show you how to take your share of what the market has on offer. The reward is always far more than the sacrifice, no matter how small the start may seem. If anything at all, simply try something and don't give up. You will deny yourself of numerous possibilities if you don't try when the opportunity is presented to you. Life can only offer so much, you are the only one who can determine how much of that will be yours.

# CONTENTS

# 1. SHOULD I OR CAN I START A BUSINESS?

*"If you wait until all the lights are 'green' before you leave home, you'll never get started on your trip to the top."*

*"Two sure ways to fail—think and never do or do and never think."*

— Zig Ziglar, *author and motivational speaker*

It is true that economies across the globe have been shaken and indeed are still trembling, to say the least. However, it is also true that in the midst of the same conditions there are countless many who seem not to be touched by the uncertainties in the economy.

Here are a few interesting facts that might give you an idea of what I am talking about.

In a report released March 9, 2010, by Spectrem Group, *"Nearly eight million families have a net worth of over one million dollars in their savings accounts, a 16% increase from 2008. The wavering economy, crippling many Americans, clearly has not affected everyone."*

A Bloomberg Businessweek article by Alexis Leondis and Warren Giles on June 22, 2010, indicated that *"global millionaires' ranks increased by about 17 percent in 2009, with the Asia-Pacific region posting a 26 percent gain, according to a report by Capgemini SA and Merrill Lynch & Co."*

In another article dated March 12, 2010, titled "World's Richest Men Do Not Know What Crisis Is," on the PRAVDA website, a Russian online business finance website, stated that *"the total number of members of the billionaire club increased from 793 to 1011. It just so happens that there is no crisis on top of the world. Only*

12% of billionaires became 'poorer' in 2009. The number of female billionaires has grown too, from 72 to 89."

Again, the Guardian business news website on April 25, 2010, had an article that stated, "*Collective wealth of Britain's 1,000 richest people rose 30%, the biggest annual increase in the wake of the economic crisis, and in the list's 22-year history. Their combined wealth rose by more than £77bn to £333.5bn, the biggest annual increase in the 22-year history of the Sunday Times rich list. The number of billionaires rose by 10 to 53.*"

These facts simply underscore the point that what seems like an economic downturn period to many is not so to others. It is of interest to note that the typical millionaire is not even a banker or Wall Street executive, nor is he or she a CEO or celebrity but rather an entrepreneur (32 percent) or professional (19 percent). Some might easily brush it off and say, "Well, these folks were already rich anyway; what stops them from making more?" However, is it also not true that "*we are all faced with a series of great opportunities brilliantly disguised as impossible situations*" (Charles R. Swindoll)? The bottom line, I believe, is this: inasmuch as most of us might not have had a hand, at least directly, in creating the economic downturn, the groups of people who seem to be oblivious to the uncertainties of the times simply decided to see things differently and take advantage of what is there with less time to worry or cry about what is not there. Orison Swett Marden, an American writer and a successful hotelier, once made a statement affirming this fact. He said, "*Don't wait for extraordinary opportunities. Seize common occasions and make them great. Weak men wait for opportunities; strong men make them.*"

It is also worth noting that while businesses are folding up, others are expanding, and others have developed the capacity to absorb the shocks these uncertain winds are blowing, not to mention the many new ones that are springing up daily.

This book is about helping you look at things and situations around you, especially in the midst of the economic downturn and uncertainties, differently. Albert Einstein once said, "*Problems* cannot be solved by the same level of thinking that created them." The book helps you creatively identify business opportunities and equip you with all the necessary tools and steps to create a way out of the uncertainties just like those making it in the current economic environment, and even better. I believe the way forward for many of us is starting out the dreams we have been nursing so long in our minds and hearts, turning them into money-making ventures. Someone once said, "Even when opportunity knocks, a man still has to get up off his seat and open the door."

The idea of going into business, for whatever reason, has been a foremost thought of many people in almost every generation. The motives behind such thoughts vary from one individual to the other: from the desire to earn extra income to just the pride of owning a business; from fulfilling a dream to challenging one's ability to make something out of this life; from having the freedom to earn what you want to running things just the way you want them; from the influence of the lifestyle of businesspeople you know or having the ability to become a solution to a given problem in society; or even just the simple thought of becoming rich.

Having said that, I believe for many in the current economic atmosphere, it is the time to boldly take a step, look up, and do something, knowing that with determination and knowledge of what you want to do, only the sky is the limit. Or you can crawl into your shell and weep, wasting away in the process. As a personal principle, I strongly believe crying over spilt milk is a waste of precious time and energy, be it losing a job or being uncertain of your current source of income. Instead of worrying and weeping, why not find a way of getting hold of another bottle of milk to use? Most of us unfortunately have lost sight of the fact that, as Alexander Graham Bell said, "When one door closes, another opens; but we often look so long and so regretfully upon the closed door that we do not see the one which has opened for us."

There are a number of issues that are continuously hampering many who could have turned their dreams into money-making ventures. So, my friend, you are not alone in dreaming. Whatever it is, keep dreaming; it costs virtually nothing to dream but takes guts and drive to make it come through.

With well over a decade in business, both nationally and internationally, and as a business consultant and a speaker, I have had the privilege of being at both sides of the table, analyzing and advising clients on the subject of going into business.

There are many ways of looking at this subject. What I want to do is to be as straightforward as possible with you to get going.

If you are among those who already have settled in their hearts, and not only in their minds, to start a business, I commend you for making such a decision. It's a great step forward, because the process of being able to make firm decisions is essential in any kind of business undertaking. As General George S. Patton, who served in both world wars said, *"Be willing to make decisions. That's the most important quality in a good leader."* This book is your best bet in making the next strategic move in this direction.

For those who haven't yet decided, I must commend you for buying this book. It will guide you in identifying opportunities in the midst of the economic downturn and in what is really involved when it comes to starting a business. Not only that, but it will also give you the needed practical step-by-step guidelines in starting it, should you finally decide in favour of starting a business.

For others, the challenge has been the thought of having to take an initiative and answering the questions of when is the right time, how do I start, what is the right approach, etc. To those, I will say keep reading on, and we will help you clearly answer such questions.

There is another group of people who started a business, now perceived to have failed. Some of this group still have that lingering desire to try again, while others might have sadly resigned to their fate. To those groups of people, I will agree with Robert H. Schuller, who once said, *"Failure doesn't mean you are a failure it just means you haven't succeeded yet,"* and Henry Ford, who also said, *"Failure is simply the opportunity to begin again, this time more intelligently."*

All said and done, it's exciting to know that all around us are endless opportunities needing to be explored and problems begging to be solved. I believe asking the right questions are a key way in opening up our minds to the unlimited potential of the human brain in solving problems and creatively thinking through situations. Edward de Bono once said, "*Traditional thinking is all about 'what is.' Future thinking will also need to be about 'what can be'.*" Business ideas are like human reproduction—they never cease to be birthed as long as there is interaction between the brain and questions or challenges of life.

As you finally decide in favour of starting your own business, let me highlight to you a few benefits that await you on this remarkable journey you are about to undertake.

## Benefits of Starting A Business

An understanding of the benefits can greatly be a source of encouragement in acting out your dream. Some of the potential benefits of going into business are:

1. You are **your own** boss. You get to be in control, directing your business the way you want it in line with your dreams.
2. You get to manage your time better to suit your personal life.
3. You have no limit on the amount of income you earn. In fact, you get to determine the pace of growth of your income in line with your capacity to produce.
4. You set your own goals, having no limit to how successful you'll want to be.
5. You have the ability to create wealth and influence society.
6. You have a reduction in personal liability, especially in the case of setting up as a Limited Liability Company. Many national governments have formally embraced the potential of the creation of small businesses and are vigorously enacting legislations daily, favouring such business owners, for the Sole proprietor as well as the private Limited Liability Company.

7.  Businesses, in many instances, are deemed to be separate entities from their owners and directors and have a perpetual existence. They can therefore be passed on to your children whereas you cannot do so with your job.

8.  By having your own business, you have a sense of ownership, destiny, and can have a better life as the business pays for these benefits. For instance, as a business grows the business can buy cars, properties, etc, for the use of its directors, and expenses are charged to the business accounts.

9.  Stemming from the above are tax liabilities, which are largely reduced because several expenses you would have paid off from your salary can be dealt with as company expenses.

10. A company can live beyond you and be able to generate income even in your old age.

11. Owning a business gives you an opportunity of a lifetime to be an employer, thus influencing positively the lives of others and society at large.

12. Through your company, you can give to various causes of your choice, charities, educational institutions, etc. Especially for those who are passionate about various charitable causes, there is no joy comparable to setting up your own business and generating the income and profits to fund your vision without being reliant on others.

## Starting A Business In An Economic Downturn

Some of you might be saying, "I understand what the benefits are; however, we are in a period of economic downturn with even threats of double-dip recession, according to some analysts, with almost all economic theories having been defied in the last few years." Both governments and businesses are scrambling for the little piece of business out there. Apart from such countries in Asia like China and India and others like Brazil and Uruguay in South America, most economies are caught up in great levels of economic uncertainties.

This is my simple answer to you. History has taught us that it is in such crises that fresh innovative ideas are born as a solution to the challenging times. Most of the billion-dollar businesses out there today were established during the Great Depression and some recessionary years of the 1950s, '70s, '80s, and '90s.

A few more interesting facts from a USA Today article affirm this point. According to the article:

- Sixteen out of the thirty corporations that make up the current Dow Jones Industrial Average started during a recession.
- Walt Disney Corporation began during the recession in 1923-24.
- Hewlett-Packard Corporation began in 1938 during the Great Depression.
- Microsoft Corporation began during the 1974-75 recession.

This article also notes that in the recession of the early '90s, 25 percent of the over-forty executives who were made redundant went ahead to start their own businesses.

To further emphasise the point:
- Two of the oldest globally recognized firms, Proctor & Gamble Co. and General Electric Co., were founded during the panic and recessionary times of 1837 and 1873, respectively.
- Burger King was founded as a franchise restaurant chain during the ten-month recession in 1953.
- Cable News Network (CNN) was founded in 1980 during a twenty-two-month recession.

*"Challenging economic times can serve as a motivational boost to individuals who have been laid-off to become their own employers and future job creators,"* said Carl Schramm, president and CEO at Kauffman.

In the current economic downturn, for instance, on the October 13, 2010, BBC News website, there was an article that stated, *"The number of new businesses set up in the UK during the first six months of 2010 was the highest amount in more than a decade. A total of 204,361 new firms were established during the period, said business support group Yoodoo, which analysed Companies House (UK body responsible for registering a business) data."*

Also, according to the Kauffman Index of Entrepreneurial Activity, in 2009, 558,000 individuals took the decision and started new businesses in the US, 4 percent more than in 2008. In a statement, it also said, "Rather than making history for its deep recession and record unemployment, 2009 might instead be remembered as the year business startups reached their highest level in 14 years—even exceeding the number of startups during the peak 1999-2000 technology boom."

Historical records indicate a trend of more people starting new businesses during recessionary times than any other period. And even many such businesses survive with some growing to become corporate giants.

Robyn Jones, for instance, was made redundant from her job in the catering division of a construction company in 1991, just as the UK went into recession. She went ahead to start and run a catering company, Charlton House Catering, turning over about £80 million in 2010, employing around two thousand people with over one hundred and fifty clients.

James Caan, a multimillionaire entrepreneur of Dragon's Den fame, started one of his most successful businesses, an executive headhunting company, during the recession of 1992 in the United Kingdom. At the time he sold the business in 1999, it had expanded into thirty different countries with one hundred and forty-seven offices. In an answer to the question of the ideal time for a business start-up, he responded, *"I think, believe in yourself, and believe in the strength of your idea, because if you truly believe that idea is a compelling proposition, it's going to work regardless. It may not be as big, it may not grow as fast but it will succeed, because good ideas always work."*

Of course there are times when conditions may seemingly present themselves as more favorable for a new business start-up. At the same time, the strength of your conviction and passion can make you ride the storms well enough to safety, should you be determined enough and be willing to make the needed adjustments on the way. Napoleon Hill once said, *"The majority of men meet with failure because of their lack of persistence in creating new plans to take the place of those which fail."*

All the facts clearly support the argument that economic downturn is not necessarily a barrier to starting a new business. Instead it brings with it some opportune conditions, which, when exploited, can be a great platform for the start and growth of a business:

1.  It is an opportunity for a new business to find its feet, allowing it to test its operational systems. By the time the economy is picked up and generated sales start to increase, the systems and knowledge will have been adjusted to operations and can cope with customer requirements efficiently. In other words, if your business can thrive in a recession, think how it will soar when the good times come again.

2.  Your potential competitors are weakened, maybe closing up or even selling out, which may also be due to early retirement. You may find an opportunity to slip into if a hole is developing in the marketplace. However, you will need to do extensive market research to test the survival of your product because the economy will eventually recover.

3.  Prices often drop during a downturn. This is the right time for fantastic deals in virtually every category, from office furniture to office supplies, land and equipment to personnel and labor. Most asset prices have been knocked down, from real estate to financial markets or even heavy equipment and construction machinery.

4.  You can hire more and better-qualified people. When all the giants are laying off staff, you can find great resources

at affordable rates. Do you want to form a professional services firm or simply hire a more qualified accountant? There are many professionals (e.g., lawyers, accountants, nurses, doctors, engineers, IT professionals, bankers, investment advisors) laid off needing a new firm to work for, most of whom are ready to take the job at much more lower pay rate.

5. You can buy everything you need at auction. A lot of re-possessions also mean large equipment, office furnishings and space, restaurant equipment, or other usually expensive large items are on offer at rock-bottom prices. For instance, you could get great deals on fleets of vehicles and trucks for a delivery service or haulage or construction company.

6. Most businesses are looking to change suppliers. Even if your prices are higher, you can come in with greater value. There is the advantage of being the new kid on the block when it comes to pitching your products and services. Many companies are desperate to find new partnerships with new companies that have a different, better, or more innovative way of delivering those products and services.

7. Most people, family and friends alike, may be a bit weary or even scared to invest more money into the stock or real estate markets. They may be willing to finance a portion of your new venture or the expansion of an enterprise that has proven itself over time. The main benefit is that they know you and have a relationship with you. Having a solid and competitive business plan that delivers real numbers stands the chance of attracting the capital you need.

8. Most suppliers are giving better credit as they seek new opportunities. Credit markets are still shaky to say the least and some virtually shut down; the B2B (Business-To-Business) credit flows are keeping money circulating out of sheer necessity. The main advantage is that all parties have more incentive than ever for finding true win-win situa-

tions that allow for cash and stock flow. When everyone is looking to survive, great deals can be executed.

9.  You can get good PR by showing you are going against the trend. The media loves aberrations, and if you are optimistic by expanding or getting into business now, you would be in that category. That means you can generate some great PR by demonstrating your "alternative" view of the market.

10.  You can find great "low money" or "no money" down deals. By simply being aware of good opportunities others have overlooked and finding deals, you could get an entire business simply by taking over a lease (along with all the equipment). Many business owners want out at any cost, meaning you can negotiate great win-win deals that allow the current owners an escape while giving you an opportunity to turn around what could be, if run right, a very viable business.

11.  In recent times with the unstable economic situation around the world, a lot of government policies have been put into place to favor the establishment of small business-es. From the US to South Africa, governments are frantically establishing measures such as making soft loans, grants, and tax breaks available to small and upcoming businesses to help curb the high rate of unemployment. Stringent regula-tory requirements are even at times relaxed for the sake of such policies to encourage job creation. There is, therefore, a lot of support to ease the initial hurdles when it comes to stepping out into business.

12.  You might have lost your job and have to do something. Sometimes, the best business decision is the one you are forced into, and the incentive as well as the need for in-come is often enough to push those previously "on the fence" to strike out on their own. In the words of Joseph Campbell, an American writer and lecturer, *"Opportunities to find deeper powers within ourselves come when life seems most challenging."* There's nothing wrong with being in this

position; it simply means there is greater urgency to do something that will start to generate income as quickly as possible.

Alvin Toffler, an American writer and futurist and once an associate editor of Fortune magazine, once said, *"To think that the new economy is over is like somebody in London in 1830 saying the entire industrial revolution is over because some textile manufacturers in Manchester went broke."*

In conclusion, *"You are surrounded by simple, obvious solutions that can dramatically increase your income, power, influence and success. The problem is, you just don't see them,"* said Jay Abraham. Open your eyes, decide to look at things differently, determine to start out something, and make a smart and informed move toward one kind of business or the other. With the right practical steps, you will get hold of your dreams and turn them into reality. *"Don't wait until everything is just right. It will never be perfect. There will always be challenges, obstacles and less than perfect conditions. So what? Get started now. With each step you take, you will grow stronger and stronger, more and more self-confident and more and more successful,"* said Mark Victor Hansen.

Read on as I help you make one good choice after the other in starting the business of your dreams and increasing your earning power and scope of influence.

# 2. SPOTTING IDEAS AND IDENTIFYING OPPORTUNITIES

*"Capital isn't that important in business. Experience isn't that important. You can get both of these things. What is important are ideas."*

– Harvey S. Firestone, *founder of Firestone Tire and Rubber Company*

You have made that all-important decision from the previous chapter to start a business. Some of you might already have a kind of business in mind at this stage, while others have yet to decide on a particular line of business. At whatever stage you are, this chapter will help you fine-tune and define clearly the way forward with what kind of business will be best for you.

Before we go any further, let me state this fact, if you believe you're incapable of coming up with ideas then you won't come up with any. You will need to put aside any negativity about yourself and your capacity to be creative. Ideas can come from anywhere, and some of the best ideas will seem quite unrealistic or impossible based on your current knowledge, experience, and assumptions.

Honestly, there is no formula when it comes to how to identify business opportunities. Being creative in your thinking, closely observing situations and scenarios, and asking the right questions are some of the best ways to start. Money-making, winning ideas are all around us; a little desire to change your circumstance, a little action, a little patience to wait when you must, a little focus, and engagement with life, and you are buzzing with one.

In the words of Brian Tracy, a self-help author, *"A major stimulant to creative thinking is focused questions. There is something about a well-worded question that often penetrates to the heart of the matter and triggers new ideas and insights."* On the other hand, Martha Stewart, an American business magnate, TV host, author, and magazine publisher with a net worth of about $638 million, gave us a little peek into her thinking, saying, *"I'm not a sponge exactly, but I find that something I look at is a great opportunity for ideas."*

Having said that, there are many ideas already out there that need great improvement to meet the growing needs of consumers. To Michael Eisner, former CEO of The Walt Disney Company, *"There is no good idea that can't be improved on."* Different cultures, weather conditions, taste, fashion, habits, and regulations from one nation, and even continent, to the other requires improving on such ideas to adapt to the new environment.

Let's now explore some of the ways that can stimulate our minds in identifying some business opportunities and ideas to take advantage of.

**Turn your hobby into a viable business**. This is where you find creative ways of making money out of your hobby. Someone may be willing to pay for it. Basing your business idea around something you enjoy doing is one of the surest ways of succeeding in that business. Passion and enthusiasm sells better than just introducing a product.

**Use existing skills from past employment.** This is where we challenge you to use your skills and experience that you acquired while working in your current or previous employment to meet the needs of a niche market. You may be able to provide a product or service being sourced by your current place of employment better than a current supplier.

**Use your personality for a business idea.** You could be a good communicator, which could suggest being a good salesperson, you could be an outstanding networker, you could be a person who makes everyone feel at home anytime anywhere, or you could be a collector of a kind, selling products online to a niche market. All these can give you a fair idea of what to do and where to start.

***Have a closer look at current social trends.*** Out of social trends could be an underlying opportunity to explore. For example, more people tend to marry later than before, so there are a lot more single parents, fashion trends, behaviors, etc. Nearly one-third of men and one-fifth of women aged twenty to thirty-four live with their parents. In an Intuit report of October 2010 "Today, half the world's population 3 billion people live in urban areas. Close to 180,000 people move into cities daily, adding roughly 60 million new urban dwellers each year." And according to Trend Watching.com "Urban consumers tend to be more daring, more liberal, more tolerant, more experienced, more prone to trying out new products and services. In 2011 and beyond, go for products, services, experiences or campaigns that tailor to the very specific needs of urbanites worldwide, if not city by city. And don't forget to infuse them with a heavy dose of 'URBAN PRIDE'."

***Provide services that make others feel good.*** Some services could help people simplify and de-clutter their lives, at the same time helping them give back to their communities. A business idea to illustrate this is "a junk clearance service," where goods collected are given to charity. You can check on such websites as www.anyjunk.co.uk and www.globalideasbank.org for more details.

**Take *advantage of current trends.*** Consumer attitudes are changing regularly. This is largely influenced by a range of factors such as current fashions, the media, advertising, and changing demographics. These changes often lead to great business ideas and, in recent years, lifestyle consultants, raw food cafés, and juice bars, to name just a few, have all provided opportunities for entrepreneurs. For instance, talk about obesity, even among children, and organic foods, and ways foods are produced has attracted some attention. People are becoming more interested in naturally produced foods, tracing it back to the source of supply, such as farmers' markets. Some people have become suspicious of traditional medicine and are turning to complementary thera-pies such as aromatherapy or homeopathy. You can have a look at www.trendwatching.com for more inspiration.

**Become a tour guide or set up a leisure business in your area.** For instance, open a tea shop for an area with high popula-tion of pensioners or in one that attracts high influx of tourists. Open an outdoor center in a rural area. Talking to your local council, tourist board, Regional Development Agencies (RDAs), or municipal assembly may give you an idea of priority areas they might already have identified due to research, policy focus, etc.

**Explore the possibility of using latest technology to cre-ate a business.** The lifestyle of the 21st century thrives much on technology, and there seems to be no end to new ones popping up each day. Facebook and Twitter, to name a few, are examples of these. www.cartoonstock.com may also offer you some ideas.

**Look into your backyard.** Identify problems and difficulties that you have experienced in getting things for your home, work, or in your leisure activities.

- Is there any service you need that is not available locally?
- Is there any part of a product that is almost impossible to obtain locally?
- Are there any issues that attract most complaints from your neighbors, friends, and even visitors to your locality?
- Are there any problems that cause you so much incon-venience and are much more costly to solve?

**Ask questions.** Listen to people's problems, hopes, dreams, and aspirations. There are often good business opportunities in solving challenges people face in their businesses or jobs.

**Sell other people's goods.** It's a known fact that many new firms start off by selling goods that somebody else produced. There are a lot of opportunities to distribute foreign goods in any given country. Distributors are being sought for all the time, with the advent of direct marketing. For example, the US Department of Commerce publishes a regular magazine listing businesses looking for facilities and distributors (this is available from all US embassies and consulates). Look at www.buyusa.gov/uk/en for more information. Chambers of commerce and other trade bodies around the world also publish regular listings of businesses seeking partners willing to manufacture under licence or to act as sole distributors.

*Research local authorities, large firms, and other public bodies in your area.* Get to know what they make and components of their raw materials that they buy from outside the area, and see if you can supply such components. You can check out www.direct.gov.uk and www.usa.gov to locate the contact details of your local council or government. See www.supply2.gov.uk for an overview of the purchasing procedure of public authorities. And, more recently, a lot more websites are being created by local and municipal assemblies publishing budget plans and general operational policies, which are all a great source for business ideas.

*Look out for potential labor shortages in your area or even overseas.* Pursuit of academic qualifications other than the more traditional vocational training left many skilled shortages for traditional trades. Most of these office workers and even professionals have retrained as plumbers, mechanics, etc, and started their own businesses because of the shortages and the financial rewards that come with it. You could investigate your area for any such possible skill shortages.

*Identify opportunities by watching the news.* Newspapers, magazines, online discussion forums, blogs, and e-zines are all fruitful sources of new and emerging trends and problems that need a solution. Small advertisement sections of local papers are a good way to get an idea of local patterns of supply and demand. Read the business opportunities sections in the national and local newspapers. Eli Broad, an American philanthropist and founder of Kaufman & Broad (now KB Home) and financial giant SunAmerica (now a subsidiary of AIG) once said, *"There is no substitute for knowledge. To this day, I read three newspapers a day. It is impossible to read a paper without being exposed to ideas. And ideas... more than money... are the real currency for success."* The following resources could be helpful.

- Newspapers and magazines in your country of residence: www.mediauk.com
- Online discussion forums: www.ukbusinessforums.co.uk
- E-zines from around the world: www.ezinearticles.com

**Copy business ideas that have taken off elsewhere?** A lot of business ideas originate from abroad and get established locally. You can pick up on a trend and be the first to offer that product or service in your local area. For example, the founder of Kwik-Fit, Tom Farmer, got the idea from the 'muffler shops' he saw on a visit to the US. The decline in the popularity of DIY led to entrepreneurs in London offering a niche service assembling flat-pack furniture for customers. Websites like www.handylocals.com may help you.

**Keep up with changes in the laws of the land.** New policies and legislations are often a rich source of new business ideas. They always generate opportunities in terms of administration and implementation. New safety or health regulation requirements may prompt the supply of parts to adapt an existing process to meet the standards, or a demand for people to provide a newly introduced service. For example, the introduction of the new Home Information Packs for buyers and sellers of domestic properties from June 2007 in the UK got people training for the Home Inspector qualification, which qualified them to carry out inspections for the Energy Performance Certificate and the voluntary Home Condition Report. Keep track of legislation from parliaments and legislative bodies locally, nationally, and around the world for information on new legislation. For examples, visit www.opsi.gov.uk and www.us.gov.

**Buy an existing business.** However, it's essential to find out why the owner is selling, even if he or she is retiring. Local papers and relevant trade magazines usually advertise businesses for sale. The following sources regularly advertise updated business opportunities: www.loot.com, www.uk.businessesforsale.com, www.daltonsbusiness.com.

**Go into franchising.** You get the independence and satisfaction of running your own venture but benefit from marketing support and an established customer base. The following web links provide more information and opportunity listings for franchising: www.franinfo.co.uk, www.franchiseexpo.co.uk, www.thebfa.org, www.whichfranchise.com.

**Identify products and services to export.** Look out for products or services that are working in your current city or country of residence and export to other countries that lack such products or services.

**Use all research tools you can find.** Surveys, consumer market research, and government statistics are all available online and are easily accessible. On the World Wide Web are ideas that you can search and explore. You could also get to know of gaps in the market and useful network opportunities. Most local libraries have countless information on this.

**Visit exhibitions and trade shows.** Major exhibitions are usually packed full of start-up ideas, mostly aimed at people who are seeking to become self-employed. Check www.exhibitions. co.uk, www.tradeshow.globalsources.co, www.eventseye.com, www.expocentral.com, and www.londonasiaexpo.com for shows across the globe.

**Work as a freelancer.** Many more people are choosing to work flexibly from home or outside the traditional employment system. As a freelancer, you can often choose to work from home or in various places to cover absent staff or to help with the peaks and troughs in established businesses. Some professional and experienced managers have set up businesses as an interim, working on short-term assignments or projects at other firms. The variety and flexibility associated with this approach to work keeps attracting more people. Check out information and job listings for freelancers at www.freelancers.net and www.freelanceuk.com.

**Invent something.** Every year, around 20,000 people in the UK apply for patents, with 20 percent of these applications made by individuals rather than businesses or institutions. Many of today's household names are the brainchild of enthusiastic individuals. Inventions from penicillin to the train all have their roots from the UK. You could get more information from the UK, USA, EU and other Intellectual Property Offices around the world by visiting www.ipo.gov.uk, www.uspto.gov, www.ec.europa.eu/internal_market/copyright, www.wipo.int, and www.patentlawlinks.com. There are companies that could also help you develop your inventions. My advice is to thoroughly research the best and get good protection and agreements before you make your idea known to them.

**Take advantage to cash in on the 'time poor.'** You could start a business that meets the needs of professional and busy people who have little time available to themselves. Many kinds of business ideas fall under this category, from simple ones such as personal shopping and dog walking to many of the Internet-based businesses such as selling items on e-bay and other auction sites for others.

**Simply improve on an existing product or service.** You could simply look out for products or services you have a passion toward to improve on their quality, value, effectiveness, efficiency, reliability, and much more.

**Launch an accidental business.** First and foremost, you create something that you'll love working on even if it never takes off and eventually becomes loved by other people. What, rather perversely, is also the best way to make sure it's something cool enough and passion-filled enough to grow that loyal audience? Build a community around it. Then, finally, try to figure out how to make some cash from it.

***Look ahead.*** What do you believe consumers will want or be looking out for in three to six months from now, a year from now, that they can't find today on the market? Future trends are a big thing these days. The Henry Ford's (Ford Motors), Sir Tim Berners-Lee (World Wide Web), Bill Gates (Microsoft PC), Steve Jobs (Apple), Mark Zuckerberg (Facebook), Larry Page and Sergey Brin (Google), and many others have and still look to project the needs of consumers ahead of time.

***Fund other people's ideas.*** You may be someone who has resources but no time to get involved in the day-to-day running of business. You could make available your cash to others who need such cash to turn ideas into successful viable businesses and share in the profits. There are so many people at both ends. There are those with great ideas but with no resources. And there are those with much cash sitting in bank accounts earning next to nothing, by way of interest, with the banks investing it for their own gain and charging all sorts of fees on the money.

***Invest in stocks.*** There are various opportunities in trading in stocks both for short-term and long-term gains. From spread betting and derivatives to simple buying and selling of shares, I have a three-part article on my blog (http://vikeinvest-life.blogspot.com/) on ground rules for investing that can help you immensely

***Write for cash.*** How about writing for cash? You can contribute to various established blogging sites and get paid. Or you could create a blog of your own, write interesting stuff, simply build a great following, and with Google Adsense, you could be on your way into making some good money. Just start by searching online for some of these sites: www.ezinearticles.com, www. squidoo.com, www.hubpages.com, and www.blogger.com.

The list above is not definitive. It should be a starting point as you think about the opportunities available to you. Many money-making ideas are yet to be explored, and with the Internet you have an almost entire globe you can potentially sell to.

Winston Churchill once said, "*During their lifetimes every man and woman will stumble across a great opportunity. Sadly most of* them will simply pick themselves up, dust themselves down, and carry on as if nothing ever happened."

Some very interesting websites to look at for some very great inspiring ideas and trends include *www.iddictive.com*, *www.entrepreneur.com*, *www.businessopportunitiesandideas.com*, and *www.trendwatching.com*.

I sincerely hope by the time you finish with this book, you will be among those who stumbled across the opportunities and got up to take advantage of them.

# 3. Steps in Developing an Idea

*"If you have ideas, you have the main asset you need, and there isn't any limit to what you can do with your business and your life. Ideas are any man's greatest assets."*

— Harvey S. Firestone, *an American businessman and founder of Firestone Tire and Rubber Company*

A good new idea is often the basis for starting up a business. From the previous chapter, we have established that you could spot a gap in the market and start a business that provides a product or service to fill it or come up with ways to improve an existing product.

Identifying an opportunity or spotting an idea is a great start. However, developing the idea into a viable product or service is a critical part of the process. Unfortunately, there are those who become so consumed by their passionate desire to start a business that it clouds their judgment in making an informed decision on the idea worth pursuing. It is not enough to fall in love with an idea and pursue it. Rather, it is necessary to assess how viable this business idea is. A viable business simply must be able to grow and be or become profitable over time and must also be able to transform itself, adapting to changing times and customer needs over its lifetime or for the foreseeable future.

Asking yourself few simple questions can make all the difference between succeeding and failing. For a business to be viable, it must have positive answers to the following basic questions:

- Does my business idea meet a specific need?
- Is it an answer to a specific question?

- Is it a solution to a specific problem?
- Can I offer something different from what may already be in existence?
- Is what I want to offer going out of fashion, trend, or being taken over by new technology?
- Is it a regulated business, and can I meet the requirements in a cost-effective way?
- Can I produce the item or provide the service at a reasonable cost?
- Can I put a price on my products or services?
- Are people willing to pay for it?
- Can I make a profit at the acceptable price or price people are willing to pay for my products or services?

Understanding the market and needs of customers and tailoring your products and services in meeting these needs is a great way forward.

With the subject of viability in mind, it is important to identify *which* business you want to start. You may start as a retail business, a wholesale business, a manufacturing business, or a service provider. You will need to also define the subject of the business. That is, *what* you will sell. The final question to answer should be *how* you will sell the product or service.

Let us consider a few steps that can help us fine-tune an idea into a full-fledged viable business idea.

***Try to learn something new every day.*** Having conceived an idea or two, it may be necessary to talk to other businesspeople, friends, neighbors, if possible, anyone who looks interesting and will talk to you about what you are considering and possibly give feedback on what they think. However, exercise a lot of discretion in knowing who to talk to. In the words of Thomas Berger, "*The art and science of asking questions is the source of all knowledge.*" Browse the web, and read magazines, books, and biographies of businesspeople, expanding your knowledge each day on the ideas.

*Keep a written record of your ideas.* Whenever you are inspired by an idea, write it down. There is no limit to the number of ideas you can write down. You are more likely to remember them and can always refer to them should you forget. Writing down any idea that comes to mind can help you differentiate between ideas. It's very important to be as specific as possible at this stage. For instance, an idea such as "A Clothing or Book Store" is different from "Online Clothing or Book Store."

*Draw a mind map.* Often, to have a pictorial view of how your idea is coming together, drawing a mind map is a very good way to go. A mind map is simply a diagram used to represent words and, ideas, linked to and arranged around a central key word or idea. It helps to generate, visualize, structure, and classify ideas. It also acts as an aid in study, organization, problem solving, decision making, and writing.

*Research other conditions out there.* Evaluate potential competition, keeping notes on what you find. A thorough assessment and market research at this stage will help you to establish whether there is a market for your product or service. Some of the questions you will want your brief market research to help you answer should be:

- Is this product or service I have in mind going to satisfy a market need?
- Who are my potential customers, and where can they be found?
- What competition is out there? Is it direct or indirect, local, national, or international?
- How distinct is my product from what is being offered by the competition?

- Can the product stand the test of changing trends or take advantage of it before it dies out?
- Does the law of the land allow for such a business to be established?
- At what prices are consumers prepared to buy my product, and can I make any profit at any stage?

**Synthesise ideas.** Put two or more unrelated ideas together and brainstorm it. For instance, setting up a bookstore to providing courier service or selling clothes online to offering a professional secretarial or accountancy service or manufacturing a new brand of fruit juice to importing rice, etc. That helps to make a firm decision on the way forward.

**Sleep on the idea.** Go away for a while, thinking of something else. Often your subconscious mind will continue to work on the problem and will come up with new ideas or refinements to the original idea.

**Talk about your ideas.** Talk especially with those close to you and who have your interest at heart. Brainstorm your idea with friends, colleagues, or staff. They can give different perspectives on the idea and may know if there is anyone else doing the same thing out there. In the words of Robert Quillen, *"Discussion is an exchange of knowledge."* Or simply write down how you would have explained your idea to another person. This helps you spot flaws or areas for improvement.

**Consider impact of new technologies.** Given the pace of technological advancement, you may need to think about whether your idea can take advantage of an opportunity created by any new technology available or even yet to be developed. An example is online trading instead of the more traditional way of trading at a fixed location.

**Consider impact of social trends.** It's also very important to consider whether social trends may affect the design or demand for your product or service. Examples are concerns about global warming and carbon footprints, or increasing demand for organic food.

***Write your business plan.*** Inasmuch as I will not insist on you writing a business plan before you start, the comprehensive guide I have provided in this book can help you realistically assess the viability and potential success of your idea and chosen business model and processes.

***Protect your idea.*** You should confine and protect your idea. Keep your idea as private as possible except, of course, with the trusted and respected individuals who are part of the process of development. It will be smart to stop talking about your idea once you have finalized on the specific one to pursue, until such time as its ready for the market and any licensing necessary to protect the idea has been secured to protect your ownership. It takes wisdom to know when to speak and when to shut up.

Whatever idea you decide on, clearly understand how you think your intended business will work. Identify who your customers are going to be, what problem you are going to solve, how your product or service is going to meet the needs, how will your customers find your product to buy, who will sell it, who will deliver it, etc. You must also have clearly stated objectives of how you intend to achieve them and succeed with it.

I hope this process has helped you fine-tune your identified opportunity. In the next chapter, we will highlight a few factors that, when taken into consideration, can help put you on "top of the game" with your idea as you enter the market.

# 4. CREATING A DISTINCTION FOR YOUR PRODUCT OR SERVICE

*"You're just anybody without your identity."*

– Grenville Main, *MD of DNA Design*

Having gone through the basic steps in fine-tuning your idea, let us look at how you are going to distinguish yourself from the existing market.

## What is your Unique Selling Point (USP)?

In the words of Tom Chappell, an American businessman and manufacturer, *"Success means never letting the competition define you. Instead you have to define yourself based on a point of view you care deeply about."*

To be able to take your share of the existing market, you will need to find a way to make consumers want what you are offering other than what already exists. Establishing your USP is very important. It should focus on how your product or service will benefit the customer and what makes you totally stand out from the competition. This can be summed up in just a few words that become something like a catchphrase of your advertising jingle. It may also be expressed as a summary of what you do and how you do it better or differently than others. Do everything possible not to be tempted to choose a phrase that becomes counterproductive because you could not fulfil the promise. Your USP also helps protect your idea in the marketplace. You can establish your uniqueness by:

- Understanding the core needs of your customers and market.
- Taking the time to discover any untapped area in your market and exploiting it.
- Taking advantage of technology and the Internet with its unlimited scope and potential.
- Taking advantage of established systems and building on them without needing to start from scratch. With a bit of adjustment, a big difference can be made to an existing business model.

Or simply ask yourself questions such as:

- What are you going to do? What is going to be your speciality or niche area?
- Who are your customers? Look at the demographics: age, gender, interests, location, national or international markets, etc.
- What do these customers want? Is it a kind of flexible service, low prices, availability of your product or service locally, trusted source, or something else that will attract customers to your business?
- How are you going to do it? Will there be something special, unusual, or significant about the way you will do business? Fast turnaround, free delivery, personal service, etc?

## Developing Your Brand Right From The Start

*"A brand is not saying what it is, it's what the customer THINKS it is."* Karen Katz, CEO of Neiman Marcus

Closely associated with USP is branding. Unfortunately, most people start their businesses with nothing of that in mind. Often when I ask clients, initial reactions tend to be to shrug it off. Some make statements like, "What has that got to do with this, my small business?" Let's face it, Nike, Microsoft, Apple, KFC, McDonalds,

Coca-Cola, Toyota, Ford, Mercedes, Walmart, Tesco, BP, Shell, and the many other established brands out there started as small backyard, tabletop, and garage businesses. I strongly encourage you to have the development of your brand at the back of your mind right from the start of your business.

Let's establish what branding really means. A brand is basically a name used to identify and distinguish a specific product, service, or business. It can also be defined as the image of the product in the market. The American Marketing Association defines it as a *"name, term, sign, symbol or design, or a combination of them intended to identify the goods and services of one seller or group of sellers and to differentiate them from those of other sellers."*

Branding is, therefore, about getting your prospects to see you as the only one who provides a solution to their problem and not just about getting your target market to choose you over the competition. Brand strategist Kerry Light once said, *"The primary focus of your brand message must be on how special you are, not how cheap you are. The goal must be to sell the distinctive quality of the brand."*

Building a brand is like building a city. As a city has a network of components such as roads, houses, libraries, and shopping centers, so does a brand. Each of the components has its own unique network but still has to fit into the ultimate plan to make the city complete. A city is planned and not built in a day. It's built one component, one day at a time. So is a brand.

A good brand, among other things must:
- Clarify your position in the business.
- Clearly deliver your message.
- Motivate your buyers and deliver on your brand promise.
- Consistently reinforce your identity.
- Confirm your credibility.
- Connect to your target potential emotionally.
- Create loyalty and enthusiasm among your consumers.

An established brand, over time, brings with it a host of benefits such as:

- Adding value to your business.
- Developing a loyalty base that cut cost on marketing and advertising.
- Increasing in your turnover.
- Projecting an image of quality in your business.
- Projecting an image of a large and established business that has also been around long enough to be well known.
- Allowing you to link together several different products in your business. As you put your brand name on every product and service you sell, customers for one product will be more likely to buy one of your other products.

The question I guess you must be asking now is, "What are the specific things that I will need to focus on at this stage to ensure I start on the right footing?"

**A memorable and easy-to-remember name.** A good brand name should instinctively be easy to pronounce, attract attention, be easy to remember, be easy to recognize, suggest product benefits and usage, suggest the company or product image, be attractive, stand out among a group of other brands, distinguish the product's positioning in relation to the competition, and be protectable under trademark law. Of course, if you have your eyes on the international market (which is what I encourage every new business to aim at by taking advantage of the enormous platform handed to us by globalization and the Internet), then you ought to be mindful of the meaning of your chosen name in other languages. Lexicon states, *"A brand name is more than a word. It is the beginning of a conversation."* You can check on the meaning of names in other languages at *www.babelfish.yahoo.com*.

**A professionally designed distinctive logo.** Symbols and images are much more noticeable than text. Diane Ackerman stated, *"The visual image is a kind of tripwire for the emotions."* The image size, quality, and colors deserve important consideration.

**A catchy phrase or slogan.**

**Professionally designed stationary.** This includes business cards, letterhead, websites, and brochures. However, it's in using them that you get people associating with it.

**Strategic advertising.** Use local and national newspapers, radio, television, web-based ads such as Google Adwords, public relations, and word of mouth.

As a new business, obviously there might not be enough money to embark on all these right from the start. However, the purpose at this stage is to have all these factors in mind so that if you can only afford the logo, you do not just do anything just for the sake of it. For instance, there are a lot of free business card offers on the Internet. However, the quality of the materials and processing are mostly below standard. A little search-and-spend will get you a professionally designed quality logo, business card, and letterhead, often offered as a complete package, which communicate value and seriousness to potential businesses and clients. Also understand that *"a brand is a living entity—and it is enriched or undermined cumulatively over time, the product of a thousand small gestures"* (Michael Eisner, Disney CEO).

There are so many aspects of branding that we can talk about under brand management. However, at this stage all I want you to consider are the benefits and how to develop your brand as you work your way through the start-up stages.

In conclusion, do all you must to be distinctive and keep repeating your message, be consistent, be persistent, evolve with the times as much as is necessary, stand for something, and be linked with something specific in the minds of your consumers, and protect your distinction.

To protect your brand, it must be properly trademarked, ensuring that other people cannot use your brand for their gain. You can trademark words, names, logos, or designs or a combination of these. A trademark will give a business an exclusive right to use the trademark and may lawfully prosecute any parties that use the same trademark in the future. For a business name to be trademarked in most jurisdictions or countries it may have to be established through actual use in the marketplace, or through registration of the mark with the trademarks office or trademarks registry in that country or jurisdiction. However, in some jurisdictions trademark rights may be established through either or both means. Please note, registering a company name with the body responsible for registering of a business in most countries, be it Companies House in the UK, Federal States Business Entity Registration Offices in the USA, Registrar of Companies in (ROC) in India, Registrar of Companies - also known as CIPRO in South Africa, Office of the Registrar General in Ghana or The Corporate Affairs Commission of Nigeria etc, does not necessarily mean that you have a trademark of your company name even though no other business can be registered as your name.

# 5. What Business Model Should I Adopt?

*"Whenever you see a successful business, someone once made a courageous decision."*

– Peter Drucker, *a writer and management consultant.*

At this stage, you can decide which one of the following business models is worth starting with. A business model is simply the plan implemented by a company to generate revenue and make a profit from operations. It includes the components and functions of the business, as well as the revenues it generates and the expenses it incurs. There are different aspects and kinds of models that a business can adopt.

Many businesses these days start with one kind of model and later decide either to combine with other models or alternate it with a different model.

Among the business models under consideration at this stage are home-based, brick and mortar, e-commerce, licensing your product, multi-level marketing, and drop shipping. There are advantages and disadvantages with each model that any new business may want to start with.

## Home-Based Business
This is where the business is set up and operated largely from the business owner's home. This model is one of the most commonly adopted by new small businesses. The flexibility, freedom, and minimal start-up cost associated with this model as well as advances in technology in respect of improved communication

tools and the Internet have made having an office at home even more practical.

## *Advantages:*

- It's easily adjustable to suit your commitments, such as family commitments.
- You can manage the size and even the growth of the business.
- It usually attracts lower start-up costs, and there is less risk. That is because you will not need to lease or buy new premises to start your business.
- There are tax benefits and business rate gains for working from home.
- You can source all other aspects of the business to other organizations, e.g., warehousing, distribution, shipping, and administrative services.

## *Disadvantages:*

- Impression on customers if people will have to be coming to your home. Maintaining consistent professional image and atmosphere can be challenging.
- Restrictions by local councils, especially if it involves human traffic, heavy vehicular transports, etc, in a residential area.
- Distractions, which also can infringe on your domestic commitments. Drawing the lines between family, friends, and business commitments can be daunting.
- If you are the type who is not self-motivated and can't handle working alone for long hours, then this model might not be best for you.

## Brick & Mortar

It's a business establishment with an actual building and address outside the home, usually with walk-in customers and inventory.

That is, starting from a designated office, store, shop, premises, etc.

**Advantages:**

- You get the opportunity to interact with people face-to-face, becoming more involved in the community you operate in.
- You get to benefit from other business facilities by virtue of your location, especially if you operate in business parks or commercial high streets zoned areas.
- Depending on the type of business, you could attract walk-in traffic by virtue of your location, adding up to what you gain through your own marketing efforts.
- You become mentally and physically immersed in running your business with no distractions and a sense of going to work each day.

**Disadvantages:**

- Higher start-up cost and risk as you may have to build, purchase, or lease your premises and office.
- The inconvenience, time, and cost of transportation to and from work each day can greatly affect productivity and family, especially in the early days of working extra hours to establish presence in the market.
- It usually requires a full-time commitment upfront to get the facility ready for business, as well as employing staff to manage it.
- If it's a retail business, you must acquire inventory to merchandize your store up front.

## E-Commerce

This model basically consists of the buying and selling of products or services over electronic systems such as the Internet and other computer networks. Web-based businesses are the norm now and not the exception any more. The amount of business transacted via this model has grown extraordinarily with wide-spread Internet usage.

## Advantages:

- This is a lower risk, lower cost business to start. You don't necessarily have to have lots of personnel, stock, and facilities, as most processes (ordering, credit card payments processing, etc) are taken over electronically.
- It is ideal for niche products. Customers for such products are usually not many. But with the unlimited marketplace offered by the Internet, even niche products could generate viable volumes.
- It allows people who would have been limited in accessing your business overcome the barriers of time and distance. This is largely because the Internet can be accessed at any time of day or night and orders placed at the convenience of the customer and in the comfort of their homes. This automatically widens the scope of your market, eventually resulting in higher turnover.
- You could do it full-time or part-time.
- You can easily control how much you want to do to suit your existing commitments, such as your day job and parental responsibilities.

## Disadvantages:

- Issues such as shipping, stock purchase, and storage, and even credit card processing, can all become headaches if you don't do them right, particularly if you are a sole trader.
- It's estimated that about a billion people access the Internet globally daily. The questions to ask are: How do I get that traffic to come to my site? How can I convert them into customers confident enough to purchase my product or service?

- Activities of hackers always looking to break into business systems can become a great headache. Technical failures can cause unpredictable effects on the total process. This means a lot of effort is needed to ensure the security features are always up to date.

## Licensing A Product

Licensing is a way of commercializing your invention. It involves signing a product licensing deal with another company, granting them the permission to make use of the intellectual property rights of your invention. It's basically the process of leasing your right to an idea or product to another business entity in return for royalty. This intellectual property right may be for a patent, trade secret, copyright, technical know-how, or a trademark. A good licensing agreement must touch on the exclusivity, market, territory, terms of royalty payments, rights to modify and combine with other products, transfer and sublicense rights, limitations on liability audits rights and reporting, prohibited uses, guaranteed annual minimum royalty, advance payment, indemnity, and termination.

### *Advantages:*

- Not much risk involved as you can work part-time on your product.
- Your expected start-up cost will be much lower because your main expense is producing a prototype of your product and testing it to make it attractive to potential licensees instead of the total cost involved in setting up an entire business to produce, market, and sell the product.
- Successfully licensing your product could result in you receiving royalties long after you've stopped working on the product. You could now have the freedom and resources to focus on your next big idea.

## Disadvantages:
- It may take some level of persistence and determination to find the right licensee. It will be much wiser not to quit your day job.
- Depending on the terms of agreement, it could take a while before you earn enough royalties. Certain agreements may require a significant quantity to be sold before you are paid anything.
- It's estimated that just about 3 to 5 percent of all patented products or ideas make it to the market, partly due to the fact that getting the product through to and negotiating with big companies can be a bit challenging.

## Multi-Level Marketing

Multi-level marketing is a business model where the businessperson or distributor buys products of an existing established business, sells them, and gets compensated or receives commission not only for sales personally made but also for the sales of others they recruit to join their distribution network. This creates levels of distributors in a hierarchy for multiple levels of compensation. The distributor markets these products directly to consumers by means of relationships, referrals, and word of mouth. A distributor has basically two responsibilities: first, to sell the company's products, and second, to recruit more distributors to join the hierarchy to sell the company's products.

## Advantages:
- Usually you do not need much to start up with. You may be required to sign up to become a member of the chain or pay a deposit for your initial consignment of goods, which is not much initially.
- This could be done from home and either full-time or part-time.
- More often than not, you are provided pre-packaged tools, products, and sales techniques to start with.

- Distributors, therefore, get the advantage of an existing profitable business and marketing plan that is already in place and easy to follow.
- It offers opportunities for personal development and growth, as most of these companies run training programs for distributors, who, in turn, get the personal satisfaction of helping others in their hierarchy succeed in the business with the leadership and developmental skills experience gained.

### *Disadvantages:*
- Not being able to sell as effectively as you originally thought, which could result in a distributor not making much from the business.
- Credibility can become an issue, especially if you start treating friends like they're customers instead of friends or vice versa.
- Building the right kind of business relationships and a profitable team is quite a process and requires a lot of time, cash, and patience.

### Drop Shipping

Another model that has recently gained popularity is drop shipping. With this model, the retailer does not keep goods in stock but takes orders and forwards customer orders and shipment details to either the wholesaler or manufacturer, who then ships the goods directly to the customer. Stocking the products is the prime responsibility of the wholesaler or manufacturer and not the retailer. The retailer makes his or her money, as in any business, between the retail and wholesale price.

### *Advantages:*
- Very little start-up cost because you may only have to consider getting a basic e-commerce website that your customers can place their orders through.

- Stocking inventory is not of your responsibility. Apart from savings from cost of storage, you also need not worry about unsold merchandise.
- You get to have a lot of time on hand to concentrate on marketing the products.
- Greater profit margin is very likely as you tend to have limited overhead cost.
- The exit strategy for this model can be quick and less costly should you decide to move on to other things.

### Disadvantages:
- Finding reliable and professional suppliers of the products you intend to sell can be quite challenging.
- There is also the problem of sold-out stocks, which a retailer may not be aware of at the time the customer orders. This may result in long waits for the customer.

As I mentioned earlier, there are so many other business models out there in the marketplace, most of which do not stand the test of time. However, the above are among the most time-tested models that you can consider as you decide on a business model to adopt for your business.

Join me for the next chapter as we consider and analyze the next most important decision to make in starting your own business.

# 6. WHICH LEGAL STRUCTURE WILL BEST SUIT ME?

*"In modern business it is not the crook who is to be feared most, it is the honest man who doesn't know what he is doing."*

— William Wordsworth, *a major English poet*

It is important to make an informed decision on the right legal structure of the business you want to set up. There are a number of legal structures, all of which differ in several aspects.

Contacting the agency responsible for registering a business in your country of residence or business interest such as Companies House in the UK, Federal States Business Entity Registration Offices in the USA, Registrar of Companies in (ROC) in India, Registrar of Companies - also known as CIPRO in South Africa, Office of the Registrar General in Ghana or The Corporate Affairs Commission of Nigeria, Department of Registrar of Companies of Botswana, Accounting and Corporate Regulatory Authority (ACRA) of Singapore, etc, is the best way forward. This way, you will get to know of the requirements and procedures necessary to get registered.

For simplification and consistency, I am adopting the United Kingdom legal structure as the basis for this chapter. However, there are quite a number of similarities in the underlying principles around the world.

Your choice of legal structure will, among other things, affect:
- Your tax liability and amount of National Insurance or Social security payment you will be liable for

- The level of risk and control you will have
- The records and accounts you will need to keep
- Your financial liability in the event of insolvency
- The transferability of the business
- The way management decisions are made in respect of the business
- The prices you charge
- The ways you can raise money for the business.

Some of the legal structures that are usually adopted include sole trader, partnership, limited liability partnership (LLP), limited liability company, franchise, and social enterprise. We will look at the common features of each structure and the advantages and disadvantages of adopting each.

## Sole Trader

This is the most common structure adopted by new business owners. It is the simplest way to run a business, as you are the only person legally responsible for the running of the business. The following are some of the features of a sole trader business:

- You are only required to register as self-employed, with no registration fee required. You register in your own name because the business is regarded as being one and the same as its owner.
- You get to make all the decisions on how to manage the business.
- Raising capital could be from your own assets, friends, bank loans, etc.
- You must also keep records showing your business income and expenses.
- Your profits are taxed as income.
- You also need to pay fixed-rate Class 2 and 4 National Insurance contributions on your profits.

- You have to make an annual self-assessment tax return to HM Revenue & Customs.

### Advantages:
- It is simple and quick to set up and run, with no registration fee required.
- Bookkeeping is quite simple and straightforward. At the end of a trading period, you are only required to prepare a profit and loss account and a balance sheet.
- You get to keep all the profit after tax.
- It is also very easy to transfer your interest to another person either by selling or by inheritance.
- You get to be able to make swift decisions, as you are not required to consult any other person for his or her input.

### Disadvantages:
- It only exists as long as the owner is alive and mentally sound to run it.
- You are also personally liable for any debts incurred by your business.
- Your home or personal assets could be used or sold in paying the debts incurred by your business.

## Partnership
This is the next most popular legal structure adopted. It is a relatively simple and flexible way for two or more people to own and run a business. However, each partner is regarded as self-employed, and there is no formal registration process with this structure. Partners usually share in the decision-making process. Here are the main features of a partnership business structure:
- A partnership has no legal existence distinct from the partners themselves.
- It is wise to have a written agreement between the partners that sets out the terms of the partnership, such as

name of partnership, nature and duration of business, capital contributions required of each partner, drawings, profits and loss sharing ratios, leave entitlements, responsibilities and restrictions on authority, retirement and expulsions, arbitrations, and notices.

- The business can be managed by the partners or by employees.
- Partners usually contribute to raise the capital either in cash, own assets or take loans.
- There can be non-active partners, who usually contribute money to the business but may not get involved in the day-to-day running of the business.
- Partnerships have to keep more detailed financial records such as sales and purchase records, cash books, creditor and debtor details, profit and loss sheets, and balance sheets. This is important both for the partnership and for legal purposes.
- The partnership and each individual partner must make annual self-assessment returns to HM Revenue & Customs.
- Profits are shared based on the partnership agreement, usually in percentages.
- Partners are taxed on their share of the profit, because they are assessed as self-employed even though they are in a partnership.
- Each partner also needs to pay Class 2 and 4 National Insurance contributions.
- If one of the partners resigns, dies, or goes bankrupt, the partnership must be dissolved, although the business can still continue.
- Partners share the risks, costs, and responsibilities of being in business.

**Advantages:**
- It is relatively quick and easy to start, even if you decide to write a partnership agreement to govern the business

relationship. Solicitors and lawyers are best able to help you with this.

- There is the advantage of complementary skills with two or more people working together, with each bringing different skills to the table.
- There is also the added advantage of being able to pull together larger amounts of resources by way of capital to be contributed.
- The demands of accountability between partners encourage better organization of the business in terms of administration and financial systems.
- Partners also share responsibility for business debts incurred with the other partners, thus lessening the burden on each individual partner.
- The records to be kept are quite simple.
- Making decisions together encourages creative brainstorming and also provides moral support to each other.

### Disadvantages:

- A partner's personal assets can be claimed by a creditor to pay off any debts, even in situations where the debt was incurred by the other partners.
- Partners are jointly liable for debts owed, and each partner is also personally liable for the whole of the partnership debts. That is, should the business fail with outstanding debts and a partner is not able to pay off his or her portion of the debts, the others will be required to pay up.
- All partners are also liable for debts incurred due to a partner's dishonesty or mismanagement without the others' knowledge.
- Decision making is a bit slower and more flexibility is required as other partners have to be consulted and negotiated with to arrive at a decision.

- Some investors find it a bit complicated to invest in partnership businesses.
- Changes in expectations and situations may result in disagreement in management plans, operational procedures, and the future direction of the business. This can cause splits among partners, especially in the case of long-term partnerships.
- There can also be disputes when it comes to valuing each other's commitment, time, and skills, if, for instance, one is coming on time to work and working so many hours a day, while the other is constantly late and never completes a task.
- Partners may also have different visions or goals for the business.
- Profits are shared, of course, according to the terms of agreement.

Partnerships thrive very well when each partner brings a specific strength to the table, each partner takes on a defined role, and there is general agreement on the vision, goals, and the business plan from the onset.

### Limited Liability Partnership (LLP)

This is a business structure that gives the benefits of limited liability but allows its members the flexibility of organizing their internal structures such as in traditional partnerships. It has some similarities with ordinary partnership, as a number of individuals or limited companies share in the risks, costs, responsibilities, and profits of the business. Professional partnerships such as accountants and lawyers favor such a structure. Some of the features of this structure include:

- A separate legal entity in its own right and can sue and be sued.

- Any new or existing firm of two or more persons can also incorporate as an LLP.
- It must be registered with Companies House at a fee.
- Annual returns and accounts are required to be filed with Companies House. Reminder letters are sent to the LLP a few weeks before the due date for filing accounts and returns.
- Each member needs to register as self-employed and file annual self-assessment returns to HM Revenue & Customs.
- There is no restriction on the number of members, but there must be at least two designated persons at all times. If at any time there are less than two designated members, then every member is deemed to be a designated member. Designated members by law have other responsibilities such as appointing an auditor, signing the accounts, and filing notification of registered office and members.
- It is good to have a written agreement that governs the partnership.
- Members can manage the business or delegate responsibilities to employees.
- Capital is raised out of members' own assets or loans.
- It can only be for making profit.
- Each member takes an equal share of the profits, unless the member's agreement specifies otherwise. Members of a partnership pay tax and National Insurance Contributions (NICs) on their shares of the profits.
- Profit of any member of an LLP is taxable as profits of a trade, profession, or vocation, and members remain self-employed and subject to Class 2 and 4 NICs.

## Advantages:
- The liability of partners is limited to the amount of money they have invested in the business and to any personal guarantees they may have given to raise the finance.

Members are therefore protected should the business run into trouble.
- There is the advantage of being a separate legal entity.
- There is a general perception that businesses with limited liability are less risky to investors and therefore it is much easier to attract investors as partners.
- Limited partners can leave the business or be replaced without the need for the limited partnership to be dissolved.
- There is flexibility in the organizational structure. Members are able to manage the business using their expertise and make key decisions, avoiding unnecessary long procedures.
- There is less public scrutiny because the partnership agreement remains confidential.

### *Disadvantages:*
- The regulatory requirements demand more formal processes even at the set-up stage and in filing of returns.
- Though the partnership agreement is not made public, other requirements such as filing of returns and accounts allows such documents to be put in the public domain, attracting scrutiny.
- Transferring a member's interest can be complicated.
- An LLP cannot be converted into a limited company.

### Limited Liability Companies (LLC)
A limited liability company is a business with shareholders whose liability is limited by shares. This is among the most common form of privately held companies. One of the major distinguishing features is that personal finances or assets of the directors are distinct from company finances. However, directors may be required to guarantee loans or credit granted to the company. There are four main types of limited liability companies:

1. Private limited companies can have one or more share-holders. They cannot offer shares to the public. The liability of each member is limited to the amount unpaid on shares that a member holds.

2. Public limited companies (PLC), on the other hand, must have at least two shareholders and must have issued shares to the public to a value of at least £50,000 before it can trade. Liability of each member is limited to the amount unpaid on shares that a member holds. A PLC may offer its shares for sale to the general public and may also be quoted on the stock exchange.

3. Private unlimited companies are rare and usually created for specific reasons. It is recommended you take legal advice before creating one. This type of company may or may not have a share capital, and there is no limit to the members' liability. Because there is no limitation on members' liability, the company has to disclose less information than other types of companies.

4. Private companies limited by guarantee. With this type of company, members do not make any contribution to the capital during its lifetime as they do not purchase shares. The members' liability is limited to the amount that they each agree to contribute to the company's assets if it is wound up, closedown or cease doing business.

Basic features common to this business structure include:
- It must be registered at Companies House.
- It must have at least one director (two if it's a PLC), who may also be a shareholder. Directors must be at least sixteen years of age.
- Shareholders may be individuals or other companies.
- Private companies are not obliged to appoint a company secretary, but if one is appointed, Companies House must be notified. Public limited companies, on the other hand, are obliged to have a qualified company secretary.

- A director or board of directors makes the management decisions.
- Directors are responsible for notifying Companies House of changes in the structure and management of the business.
- It is financed by shareholders' contributions, loans, and retained profits.
- Public limited companies can raise money by selling shares on the stock market, but private limited companies cannot.
- Limited companies exist in their own right. This means the company's finances are separate from the personal finances of their owners.
- Accounts and records are required to be kept and must be filed with Companies House before the time allowed for filing those accounts to avoid a late filing penalty.
- An annual return must be filed yearly, at a fee, updating Companies House with basic details relating to the company.
- Accounts must be audited each year unless the company is exempt.
- Profits are usually distributed to shareholders in the form of dividends, apart from profits retained in the business as working capital.
- If a company has any taxable income or profits, it must tell HM Revenue & Customs that it exists and is liable to corporation tax.
- Company directors are employees of the company and must pay both income tax and Class 1 National Insurance contributions on their salaries.

### Advantages:
- Shareholders or members are not personally liable for the company's debts. Only the assets of the LLC can be used to pay off business debts. However, directors may

become liable for business debts by providing personal guarantees in securing loans to the company.

- It has a separate legal entity and can sue and be sued. It is completely separate from its members.
- For a lot of businesses, and even in some industries, being incorporated as a limited liability company provides the professional image a lot of customers like to associate with.
- The name of your business is protected by law once it is registered with Companies House. No one else can use the registered business name.
- An LLC, especially a PLC, may find it relatively easier to secure business funding as it can issue various classes of shares to the general public.
- It is much easier to transfer ownership of a limited company, usually by means of transferring ownership of shares held.
- An LLC can fund its employees' pensions as legitimate business expenses rather than paying for it out of tax-free income.
- A private limited company is likely to pay less personal tax than a sole trader. Directors and shareholders of a private limited company may elect to take small salaries and take most of their income in the form of dividends because dividends are taxed separately and are not subject to National Insurance.

### Disadvantages:
- The formation of LLCs has more requirements than a sole trader or a partnership.
- Registration is not free. Registering directly with Companies House may not be expensive; however, professional fees for putting together other documents such as memorandums and articles of association may add to the overall cost.

- Regulatory requirements on public filing of returns and accounts means exposing company information and details for public scrutiny, including customers and competitors.
- Proper accounting records must be kept and, if you are over the audit threshold, you will need to pay auditors to audit your books.
- Because of the limited liability clause, lenders may ask directors to personally guarantee the loans. That raises the question of 'how limited is your liability' in the event of business failure.
- There is also the issue of takeover threats from other businesses. This is because almost anyone can buy enough shares and persuade other shareholders to join them in their bid, especially in the case of public limited liability companies, to take over the business.
- In public companies, shareholders' expectation of steady streams of income may mean concentrating on short-term objectives to make profits, whereas focus on longer term objectives of growth and investment would have yielded higher and better returns in the future.
- Private limited companies cannot sell their shares to the public. It, therefore, limits its ability to raise more capital for expansion should the need arise.

**Franchise**

Franchise is one of the business paths you can take if you are the type who is more comfortable with already tried and tested structures and systems, because with this type of structure, you buy a licence to use the name, products, services, and management support systems of the franchising company. It brings together the talents of the new business owner with the experience, knowledge, and track record of the franchiser. You are, therefore, granted the right to market an already established company's goods or services. You get to do business using the marketing methods, trademarked goods and services, and the goodwill and brand name already developed by the company within a certain geographical area. There is a common saying that with a franchise you are in business for yourself but not by yourself.

Many different types of business sectors use this structure. The most common franchised businesses are found in the food and drink industry. Examples include McDonalds, Subway, Starbucks, and Pizza Hut. However, other industries, such as hotel and travel, automotive, financial services, and cleaning and maintenance services, also operate under this business structure.

Common features of a franchise business include:
- The license normally covers a particular geographical area.
- It runs for a limited time, after which it can be renewed, as long as it meets the terms of the franchise agreement.
- Franchises may be paid for through an initial fee, ongoing management fees, a percentage of turnover, and purchases of goods from the franchiser, or a combination of these.
- It can take different legal forms. Most of them operate as sole traders, partnerships, or private limited companies.
- The franchisee's freedom to manage the business is limited by the terms of the franchise agreement.
- Franchise agreements usually set out how the franchised business should be run, although they may allow some flexibility. Franchisers usually provide management help and training to franchisees.
- Franchisers often expect franchisees to show them detailed financial records as well as the usual legal requirements as a business entity.
- The amount of tax and national insurance to be paid is dependent on the business structure that the franchisee chooses for his or her business.

### Advantages:

- The business is based on a proven idea. The franchisee can always confirm the success from existing ones.
- The franchiser company usually offers full training and ongoing support in all aspects of the business to the franchise owner.
- There is a "ready made" time-tested operating system in place to be adopted, with some degree of flexibility in some cases.
- The franchiser usually grants exclusive rights to the franchisee within a specific geographical area and normally will not sell another license to within the same territory.
- An already established brand name makes it easily recognizable and accepted. Consumers are more comfortable with buying from a familiar name or business.
- Often, marketing tools and advertising campaigns are provided, to the benefit of the local franchisee business.
- Franchisees also benefit from great discounts, as they are able to buy in bulk through a centralized purchasing system.
- Financing a franchise business with a good brand name can be much easier as banks may already have seen the viability of such a business.

### Disadvantages:

- Buying a franchise license can be costly. You may also have to pay continuing royalties after the initial cost of the license. And often pay a percentage of your turnover to the franchiser. This obviously affects the overall profits of the business.
- The license may also include restrictions on how the business is to be operated. This may limit creativity and adaptability to a unique area.

- There is a huge uncertainty and risk should the franchiser be taken over or collapse altogether.
- To sell your license to another is not easy as it will be subject to the franchiser's approval.
- Other badly operated franchisees could give the brand a bad name, which can be very difficult to rectify by your good service or quality product.

A good and thorough research of the franchiser business before starting and your ability to work just as hard as your brand is working for you are the keys to succeeding in this business.

## Social Enterprise

These are businesses with primarily social and environmental objectives. The authorities define them as "businesses with primarily social objectives whose surpluses are principally reinvested for that purpose in the business or in the community, rather than being driven by the need to maximise profit for shareholders and owners."

## Basic features include:

- There are many different types of social enterprises, including community development trusts, housing associations, worker-owned co-operatives, and leisure centers.
- It is not established for a profit-making purpose. Profits are to be reinvested in the business or in the community rather than given to shareholders and owners.
- They take a number of different business structures; the most common are companies limited by guarantee, companies limited by shares, and industrial and provident societies.

## *Advantages:*

- They are usually tax-free.
- Some get funding support from various government agencies.

- People who identify with the business's course often tend to give to support the enterprise's activities.
- It has more flexibility in its style of operation and internal structure.

### Disadvantages:

- Financial institutions do not normally lend to such businesses. It can only raise money by approved means, which are usually freewill giving from its members and donations from the general public.
- Trustees may be liable, especially in cases of misappropriation of funds.
- Structures of such businesses can be unclear, which tends to hamper the smooth running of the enterprise.

Deciding in favor of any of the above structures is very necessary for now and for the future survival and growth of your business. Failing to adopt the best structure in the light of your needs and aspirations may lead to disappointments, especially when the tax man comes after you or you find yourself in a legal suit. In the event of your business turning out profits without a properly adopted structure, the tax man is left to decide for you what is due him, and that can wipe away a lot of your hard-earned gains. On the other hand, in the event of a business failure, your liability can seriously affect your person. You could also lose out on benefits, such as writing off certain expenditures as business expenditures and other benefits you could have taken advantage of as a new or small business.

As you can see, it is in your interest to make a firm decision based on the features, advantages, and disadvantages I have provided for your consideration.

# 7. PROVEN WINNING STRATEGIES FOR GROWTH

*"Change is not a destination, just as hope is not a strategy."*

> — Rudy Giuliani, *an Italian American lawyer,*
> *businessman, and former Mayor of New York City*

*"Sound strategy starts with having the right goal..... Strategy is about making choices, trade-offs; it's about deliberately choosing to be different....The company without a strategy is willing to try anything."*

> — Michael Porter, *Professor at Harvard Business School,*
> *and a leading authority on company strategy and*
> *the competitiveness of nations and regions*

A business strategy clearly helps you to articulate the direction a business will pursue and the steps it will take to achieve these goals. A good strategy should clearly differentiate a business from its competitors. Adopting or crafting a better strategy helps a business establish a clear framework for subsequent decisions, giving a business an edge in the marketplace right from the start. Your understanding of these strategies will help you choose the winning approach to success.

In this chapter, we will discuss marketing, pricing, advertising, and sales strategies as core strategies that need serious consideration for you to succeed in business. However, the growth and increasing potential of social media as a marketing tool cannot be glossed over. I will briefly discuss a few important facts you need to know in taking advantage of this.

## Marketing Strategy

Marketing is essentially about getting the right product or service in front of the people who will want to buy that product. A marketing strategy helps you identify and communicate the benefits of what your business offers to your target market, whereas a marketing plan helps you to simply implement your marketing strategy. A good marketing strategy should help you address the specific needs of the different customer groups. Contents of the marketing strategy should be measurable and actionable and work to differentiate your company and products from the competition. The objectives of your marketing strategy should also establish specific goals, such as, "Our goal is to capture 10 percent of the existing market in the next twelve months and 25 percent by the end of three years in ten cities," or, "We want to achieve a turnover of £1 million in the next two years within the southwest region." It must also take into account how your business strengths and weaknesses will affect your marketing.

A workable strategy should help you; identify the specific customer segments you are targeting and your positioning in that market segment; identify how to serve your targeted customer segment or group, i.e. define the benefits they are looking for and how you intend to deliver to meet that, and the technology you intend to use; establish your marketing objectives, such as your intended market share, growth, how you intend to enter the market, and how you intend to increase awareness of what you are offering; and, work out what mix of marketing tools such as products, price, place, and promotion you will use to help you deliver the needed benefits to your customers and beat the competition.

Answering the following questions can help you create a good basis for putting a workable strategy together:

- How do you define what your company is?
- What are the products or services your company will provide?
- Who are your target customers?

- Which marketing category will you establish yourself in?
- Does your company intend to become a market category leader, challenger, follower, or niche player?
- What are the unique characteristics of your products or services that distinguish you from the competition?
- What are your pricing policies? Will your price be above, below, or at parity with your competitors, and are you going to lead, follow, or ignore changes in competitors' pricing?
- Through which distribution channels will your products or services be made available to the target market?
- How will your advertising and promotions convey the unique characteristics of your product or service?
- Which research and development activities or market research plans are unique to your business?
- How can you describe the image or personality of your company and its products or services?

One of the most commonly used marketing strategies by new and small businesses is the growth strategy. The focus of this strategy is to simply help you identify the way you will use products and markets or customers to achieve a desired level of growth in your business. Here are some growth strategies:

**Current product for current market.** This strategy is used to increase your share of an already existing market. It is usually implemented by finding new customers or raising customers' awareness of your current products and services.

**Current product for new market.** This is a strategy of finding and entering new markets with your current product or service. This new market could be a new segment of the market, a new country, or a new region.

**New product for current market.** This strategy approach simply demands you improve your existing products and services or develop new ones to enhance the benefits you deliver to your customers.

*New product for new market.* This strategy involves adopting new ways of doing business, which could carry higher risk and cost. It's more than simply offering new products or services in a new market. There is a bit more risk involved in adopting this strategy because you are more or less charting an uncharted territory, with totally new products for an entirely new market.

Marketing strategy can only benefit your business strategy if you use it. It is also important to ensure that you have the operational capacity and processes for fulfilling any extra orders, ensuring timely delivery, and providing any extra services efficiently and reliably in handling the extra business your strategy generates.

## Pricing Strategy

Pricing strategies are sometimes not given much consideration by new businesses. However, they are a major determining factor in the survival or success of a business and a workable component of a good marketing strategy. Understanding this strategy and getting it right will positively affect your revenues and profit. For some businesses, it's simply looking at what is being charged by competitors and setting prices accordingly. A lower or higher price can significantly change both sales volumes and gross margins and, subsequently, profits.

Understanding some of the factors that influence how much people are willing to pay for goods and services will be very helpful at this stage. People generally pay a price based on the:

- Price of substitute products or services in the marketplace.
- Price of related products or services available.
- Cost of the problem a product or service solves.
- The status associated with using or owning such a product or service.
- Cost of a problem the product or service prevents.
- Location where the product or service is provided.
- Persons using the product or service.

- Revenues that can be generated from owning the product or service.
- Customer service and support provided both before and after the service or product is sold.
- Guaranteed warranty period.

Establishing your pricing objectives is undoubtedly among the most basic and important things to do. However, you can only accomplish the stated objectives after taking the following factors into consideration.

**Cost of production.** It is critical to take into account both the variable and fixed cost components of producing a product or providing a service. Variable cost is the cost that changes according to the change in the volume of production. Fixed cost, on the other hand, does not change unless there is a major expansion of the business. A pricing policy should cover both types of cost for the business to turn a profit.

**Position in the market.** It is important to determine if pricing is going to be a key factor in positioning yourself in the market. Positioning your price as an exclusive luxury product, for instance, demands a different approach than operating as a discount store. Whereas the discount store has to keep its prices as low as possible consistent with its objectives, pricing an exclusive luxury product too low may rather hurt the product's image. Pricing should, therefore, be consistent with the positioning of the product in the market. The idea of "you get what you pay for" subconsciously has some level of influence on how the price of a product is perceived.

**Demand of the product or service.** Good basic market research should help you determine how your price will affect the demand of your product. Asking potential customers how much they will be willing to pay at each price can help you decide the price that can give you the right balance of higher turnover. A simple questionnaire asking how much respondents are willing to pay for a service or product at various prices can help, especially in the case of small, new start-up. A larger firm or one with more resources may be able to hire a market research company.

***Environmental factors.*** It is equally important to find out what external factors may affect your pricing strategy. It is important to consider the implication of your pricing on your competitors. To set a price too low may be inviting an unpleasant risk of price wars. On the other hand, setting a price too high may attract a large number of competitors who want to share in the profits. Legally, a firm might not have total freedom in setting its price at any level. For instance, pricing too low may be considered predatory pricing, offering different prices for different consumers might be seen as price discrimination, or colluding with competitors to price a product or service may be illegal, which it is in most economies.

The above factors should help you establish what your pricing objectives must be. The objectives could be:

- Seeking to maximize profit in the short run. This is not a very good objective if it results in lower long-term profits.
- Seeking to maximize current revenue with little regard for profit margins. This enables a business to increase its market share and lower cost now to ensure long-term profitability.
- Reducing long-term costs by maximizing the number of units sold or the number of customers served to increase profit in the long run.
- Maximizing profit margins on each unit of item sold. This is used particularly for items or products that are sold in small quantities, such as handmade automobiles and artwork.
- Using the price to signal high quality or a high level of service in an attempt to position the product as the quality leader. At the other extreme is to be the low-cost leader as a way of differentiating yourself from the competition.

- Surviving by covering just the cost. This is used especially when the market is in decline or over capacity.
- Seeking price stabilization just to avoid price wars and maintain a moderate and stable profit margin. Many new businesses do this.

With the understanding gained from the objectives and factors that should be considered in determining the price of a product, let us now look at some pricing methods you may adopt. However, it is important to establish that there is no one right way to price a product or service.

*Cost-plus pricing.* This is among the most common methods. The price is set at total cost of production plus a certain profit margin. Always remember that the cost of production includes both fixed cost and variable cost at the current volume.

*Target return pricing.* This means setting a price to achieve a return on investment. You want to recoup your investment within a certain time frame by pricing your product to achieve that set investment target.

*Value-based pricing.* With this method, you set the price based on the value of the product or service to the customer. This is used especially when the product or service significantly saves more for the customer.

*Psychological pricing.* The price is set based on factors such as what a consumer perceives to be fair, popular price points (the price at which people are much more willing to buy a certain type of product) and signals of product quality (are you a low-cost leader or high quality product or service provider?).

Finally, let me tie all the above together and give you a shot at some of the best strategies worth considering.

*Cost plus mark-up.* With this strategy, you decide the profit you want to make and add it to your cost to determine your selling price.

*Competitive pricing.* This is the opposite of cost plus mark-up. With this strategy, you use your competitors' prices as benchmarks to price your products or service. You could decide to price your products slightly above, below, or as your competitors, depending on your positioning strategy.

*Trade discounting.* This strategy seeks to attract business from profitable customer category (i.e. customer segment who contribute most of your profits) offering those special discounts, either as lower prices on certain products or free product rewards.

*Loss leader.* This involves selling below cost in order to attract more customers with the belief that they will buy other high-profit items. This is one strategy commonly used by most supermarkets.

*Bundling and quantity discounts.* This is where customers are rewarded for higher purchases through bundling or quantity discounts. It is done by setting the per-unit price lower should a customer purchase more instead of one, or charging less when a customer buys several related items in a single shopping trip.

*Versioning.* This is where you sell a general product in different configurations so the basic version is either offered free or at a very low price and the other services are available at a higher price.

*Close out.* This is best used when there is excess inventory to get rid of. The goal here should be to minimize losses instead of making profits. Stocks are sold at steep discounts to reduce or avoid storage cost.

Good pricing requires good market research. Find people who will be potential customers of your products, understand their needs and provide what will meet their needs. Settle that, and determine your price based on your pricing objectives and existing or applicable factors to ensure the growth and profitability of your business. It is equally important to focus on adding value to your products as much as possible instead of relying solely on pricing in making your product much more competitive.

## Advertising Strategy

*"Nothing except the mint can make money without advertising."*
Thomas B. Macaulay

Every business needs to promote itself constantly in a way to reach out to its customers and potential customers. Advertising is basically the methods used by a business to publicize and position its products and services to its target market. This includes the use of salespeople, product launches, brand name and image, promotion of the product in retail and wholesale outlets, press releases and other public relations activities, and special offers.

An advertising strategy must support your marketing strategy. The aim is to attract the customer, capture his or her attention, and leave an impression of interest and some level of curiosity.

*"Good advertising does not just circulate information. It penetrates the public mind with desires and belief."* Leo Burnett.

It may be the only way customers form their first impressions of your business until they ever buy from you. You must use different ways of thinking and creative strategies to create slogans, sounds, and impressions that will communicate the information you want to send to your intended audience.

*"Advertising says to people, 'Here's what we've got. Here's what it will do for you. Here's how to get it'."* Leo Burnett

Just stop with me for a moment and consider this. As we embark on our daily routines, we see or hear of something being advertised. It gets our attention and, if it's of relevance to us, we get interested. If it has a resemblance to what we need or have been thinking about, what do we do? We desire it and even plan how we will own and use it.

A good advertisement should, therefore:

- Generate awareness of your business.
- Provide basic information on your business contact details.

- Result in increased sales by letting your potential customers know about your product or services.
- Inform customers about latest offers, new product launches, and improvements to your services and products.
- Make you stand out, creating a distinctive brand for your business and establishing you as the first choice for customers.
- Enable you develop a unique position and niche in the market.
- Be attractive enough to cause suppliers to want to do business with you and even entice potential employees.

A well-planned advertisement will have long-range benefits for any small or new business. Let's look at some of the methods or mediums by which you can advertise your business.

**Word of mouth**. Spread the word among relatives, friends, colleagues, and former colleagues who will tell others, and others will tell others, and on and on.

**Your voicemail**. As interesting as it may sound, changing the message on your voicemail to reflect the fact that you are now in business for yourself is a simple great start.

**Business cards.** Have them professionally designed with a touch of excellence and quality. Never be without them and hand them out at every opportunity.

**Flyers.** There are many places (local groceries, libraries, cafes, etc.) that will allow you to display your flyers freely.

**Website:** Create a website, which is almost free to do these days. Or you can get professionals to do it for you at very little cost. Advertise your site to the world on the Internet via Google Adwords. A website helps you centralize all your business and gives you somewhere to send people to buy from you. Place your web address in your e-mail signature.

**Signs and stickers.** Bumper stickers and magnetic signs on your car is another way to go.

**Clothes.** Wear your ads by putting them on your t-shirts, sweatshirts, baseball caps, pens, etc.

**Direct mailing.** Place your business cards and flyers in your outgoing mail.

**Free classifieds.** There are a lot of free classifieds websites on the Internet that will help you place your advertisements for free.

**Send promotions with invoices.** Sending promotional materials with invoices, asking recipients to "refer a friend" is a great way forward.

**Yellow pages.** A lot of people also rely on the yellow pages to find businesses.

**Newspapers.** Local and national newspapers, besides business ad spaces, often offer special ad features for new and small businesses to advertise their products and services.

**Magazines.** Choose a magazine that your intended target market subscribes to and place an ad.

**Professional and business groups.** A lot of such bodies have exclusive advertising opportunities for its members, from free listing on their websites to inclusion in their directories.

**Radio.** Advertising on a local radio station is another approach that must be taken advantage of as it tends to be effective and much less expensive than TV and even some newspapers.

**Bus stop bench.** Advertising on benches in public areas and active bus stops is another way of advertising.

**Vehicles.** Ads can be placed on your vehicle, from custom graphics to magnetic signs on top of vehicles to removable magnetic signs that can be taken off anytime you want.

**Trade show participation.** Trade shows put together by local business associations and other similar organizations are usually much cheaper to take advantage of than nationally organised commercial and international shows.

**Email.** Mailing lists generated by your business via surveys, customer feedback, etc., can be used to advertise your products or services.

**Community involvement.** Getting involved in your locality either as a business or citizen is a very effective way of making yourself known to potential customers.

**Join other businesses.** Joining resources with other businesses can greatly work to your advantage. You can do so with complementing businesses.

**Local council website.** Advertise on websites that provide business information for your local areas. Many local councils and municipalities have local business listing pages on their sites for small businesses.

**Local and national TV ad.** Small and local TV stations have promotional offers for small businesses, from documentaries to being featured on business news, all within the budget of small businesses.

You are most likely not going to be effective by using *all* the above methods. Your best shot will be to assess your advertising needs and choose the best option (some of which are almost **free**) with your objectives and budget in mind.

Here are ten principles that can guide you in getting the best of effective advertising:

1. Use one message that is simple, catchy, short, easy to remember, and consistent. It must personally communicate to the individual reader. In the words of William Bernbach, a former advertising director, *"Advertising doesn't create a product advantage. It can only convey it."*

2. Give your ad a relevant headline other than the name of your business. *"If your advertising goes unnoticed, everything else is academic."* William Bernbach

3. For effectiveness, focus and create unique ad messages for each specific audience or target group.

4. The message must communicate the benefits of what you are offering. Ensure your advertisement avoids bold claims that your product or service cannot deliver. *"Telling lies does not work in advertising."* Stanislaw Lec

5. Create an ad that generates curiosity for customers to want to know more, even more than selling a product or service. In the words of Theodore Parker, *"Kodak sells film, but they don't advertise film. They advertise memories."*

6. All ads must have your contact details, such as telephone and fax numbers, e-mail addresses, websites, and company address, displayed very visibly.

7. Do not advertise via any medium just because your competitors are advertising in that medium.

8. Your ad must call its audience to take an action and show them where to start.

9. Negotiate with advertising houses based on what you pay for readership and audience, not just on what is quoted.

10. Constantly evaluate and test the effectiveness of your ads, and stop using a medium or method if it's not working. In the words of David Ogilvy, *"Never stop testing, and your advertising will never stop improving."*

To be very effective with your advertising strategy, you need to consciously plan for it, choose the best methods or mediums, and constantly assess each one's effectiveness. You advertise to introduce your product or service, but the quality of your product is what brings the returns. In the final analysis, as Jef I. Richards says, *"Advertising is totally unnecessary. Unless you hope to make money."*

## Sales Strategy

*"Selling is a skill to master. You will ALWAYS be selling no matter what you do. "Karen Katz"*

As a new business, your commitment and enthusiasm to what you are going to sell is essential for your survival in the marketplace. Your ability to market your products and services will determine the success or failure of the business; however, for that to be possible, you must be able to sell effectively to generate revenues and profits.

A sales strategy is not the same as a marketing strategy. Your marketing strategy should enable you make yourself known to your market and get customers to be keen on what you are offering, and your sales strategy should help you "close the deal" with your customers. A sales strategy, properly implemented, should generate increased sales and enable you effectively establish yourself in the competition.

For a sales strategy to be relevant, it is important to have different sales strategies for each of your product lines, being conscious of the different customer groups or segments you will be selling to. Here are a few steps that can guide you in putting together an effective sales strategy.

**Set objectives.** To start with, you must have objectives for your sales strategy. These objectives must be specific, measurable, achievable, realistic, and time-sensitive (SMART). Your focus can be on specific products or client groups.

**Establish features and benefits.** You must also distinguish clearly the unique features of your products and services and the benefits your customers will gain from buying them. Consider the product from your customers' perspective, and emphasize the different features from the benefits.

**Understand competition.** You need to also understand what your competitors are doing and how they are doing it. Evaluate their methods and establish what you can and should be doing differently.

**Define target market.** A clearly defined target market is a must to enable you sell strategically to generate revenues. Constantly evaluate your customer groups or segments, and design specific strategies to use in selling your products or services to each of them.

**Choose sales methods.** You must now decide which sales methods to use to reach out to the various groups, after identifying them and establishing the benefits your products will bring to them. The nature of product you are selling and the geographical area should also help you determine which method will best enable you get to the customer to "close a deal." Some of the sales methods to use include direct face-to-face selling, telesales, Internet, and direct mail.

**Present products well.** It is very important to put resources and effort into how you are going to present your products or services to your customers. There is a popular saying that "you get what you see."

**Have flexibility to negotiate.** There must be a level of flexibility in your selling approach. You will need to be able to spot opportunities for the long term and be willing to cut down on your profit margin now by lowering your prices for repeat sales as well as promotional benefits.

**Close the deal.** This is where you persuade your customer, highlighting their need or want of what you are offering. It must not stop there. You must get a firm commitment, taking note of the ensuing negotiation, particularly listening to what the customer is saying.

**Follow up.** A good rapport with a customer should be a stepping-stone in following up on the sale. Follow-up confirms to the customer your faith in the product and the integrity of the benefit and features you sold to them. Requesting customer feedback can give you a clear insight into the exact mindset of your customer and can also give you further ideas for improvement on your product or service.

## Using Social Media For Business

The use of social media has become very prominent in marketing products and services in the last couple of years, and I challenge you to explore it. It can be used to complement other methods of marketing and advertising without necessarily interfering with other mediums or methods. The benefits can be tremendous, but must be used in the most efficient way possible because not every business has the resources (time and money) or is ripe for marketing and advertising via this medium, at least not from the onset.

Businesses simply sign up for any of the social media available, such as social networking websites, blogs, or video and photo sharing websites, and build a following over time to gain much-needed visible popularity and introduce the business to followers or subscribers.

Among the benefits is the potential of being able to attract a more targeted segment of Internet users, enabling you get the needed local and global exposure and also helping you build a brand around your product or service.

Reported scams and spams on the Internet have created a kind of weariness among Internet users. However, the use of social media can provide a more personal touch in attracting potential customers.

Given that practically anyone who can use the Internet can sign up on a social network website, it requires almost no special skills in its usage. Because signing up to join most of the websites and forums are free, it's one of the cheapest ways of marketing, and the return on investment, when used effectively, can be very high. This should be great news for any new and even existing businesses with tight budgets.

The use of Facebook, Twitter, and other social networking sites to connect and interact with customers is increasingly growing in a more personalized way. Most organizations' use of Twitter, such as JetBlue, Starbucks' use of Facebook, and Honda Japan's promoting on social networking site Mixi, are clear examples of such methods.

JetBlue's, a low-cost American airline, promotion on Twitter has generated about 1.6 million followers who are constantly seeking to know about special deals for tickets. JetBlue is now able to reduce its reliance on expensive, traditional, paid media to deliver timely coupons at a minimal variable cost, enabling it to also develop a closer relationship with its consumers.

Starbucks, on the other hand, announced in July 2010 that its Facebook fan base exceeded 10 million people. It indicated that its recent strong performance is linked to this. It uses innovative ideas such as "My Starbucks Idea," a website where people can freely suggest ways to make the company better.

Honda Japan's promotion on social networking site Mixi has over half a million registered members seeking for information about the launch of one of their newest car models, CR-Z. The company creatively automatically added "CR-Z" to its users' Mixi login names, with a chance to also win a car. That created a kind of buzz, where unregistered members were curious to know why people suddenly had login names incorporating "CR-Z." Honda Japan reported that its prelaunch orders went up to 4,500 units and sales went up to 10,000 units in the first month of sales.

Using social media has basically become the online version of word-of-mouth marketing. Using it in the right way potentially will result in more customers, increased sales, and, thus, profit and growth and continuity of the business.

# 8. QUALITIES OF SUCCESSFUL BUSINESS PEOPLE

*"Whenever an individual or a business decides that success has been attained, progress stops."*

— Thomas J. Watson, *a former President of International Business Machines (IBM), who developed IBM's renowned management style and corporate culture*

I have yet to come across a person in business who does not aspire to succeed in his or her chosen business. However, the desire to succeed is not a guarantee to becoming successful. There are certain characteristics and attitudes that distinguish those who have succeeded from those who are simply surviving. Not possessing any of these qualities does not in any way disqualify you from starting out. I believe most of these qualities can be developed over time should you set your mind to it. Choices, not circumstances, determine your success. Here are some of the qualities for your consideration.

**Desire.** To succeed, you have to have an above-average desire to break out of the 9 to 5 grind, to step off the employee-job-salary treadmill, and to put your ideas, ideals, and beliefs into action. Eric Hoffer stated, *"It sometimes seems that intense desire creates not only its own opportunities, but its own talents."* An entrepreneur's desire for personal fulfilment and professional success is his or her number one key strength and that which will force him or her to start out in business in the first place. In the words of Napoleon Hill, *"When your desires are strong enough, you will appear to possess superhuman powers to achieve."* Success can only be yours if you desire enough to act to achieve it.

**Passion.** To be successful in business, you need to be passionate in what you are doing or intend to do. John Maxwell said, *"A great leader's courage to fulfill his vision comes from passion, not position."* Passion generates energy and excitement for the task ahead. Setting out to go into business on your own is a great decision but can be challenging, especially in the initial stages. Unless you are passionate about what you have on offer, you may not get anyone to want to pay for it, let alone survive to succeed in it.

**Purpose.** Successful business people have definite purpose or goal in life, know what they want, and pursue it until they get it.

**Decision making skills.** Peter Drucker once said, *"Making good decisions is a crucial skill at every level."* However, successful businesspeople take this to another level by being able to make quick decisions when it's required and sticking by those decisions. Most of these decisions are made not only based on facts but also based on what they believe in or with their instincts.

**Creative imagination.** Successful businesspeople are always creatively imagining scenarios and events well ahead of time. They always seek to have a peek into the future for ideas and solutions.

**Leadership abilities.** To be successful is equal to being able to lead yourself and others to fulfilling a desired dream or goal. A leader leads by example, whether intentionally or not. John Maxwell, a leadership expert, speaker and author, said, *"A leader is one who knows the way, goes the way, and shows the way."* Also, in the words of John Quincy Adams, *"If your actions inspire others to dream more, learn more, do more and become more, you are a leader."*

**Self-starters.** To be successful in business, you need to have the ability to take the initiative and work independently to develop your ideas. Often, even the closest of friends and family may not see what you are seeing. Do not wait on their approval and support before you set off because it may never come. People rather jump on board only when they see you start.

**Higher goals.** Successful businesspeople are mountain climbers who, having climbed one peak, look beyond to the next highest. They are resourceful and proactive. Rather than adopting a passive "wait and see" approach, they constantly set higher goals.

**Self-determination.** Successful people have strong determination to make things happen. A successful businessperson has the belief that the outcome of events is down to his or her own actions, rather than based on external factors or other people's actions.

**Judgment.** To succeed in business, you need to be open-minded when listening to other people's advice, while bearing in mind your objectives for the business. You should have the ability to listen to other people's ideas without feeling intimidated or threatened.

**Self-confidence.** As a successful businessperson, you will need to have a self-belief and passion about your product or service. Your enthusiasm should win people over to your ideas.

**Seek solutions in the face of problem.** Successful businesspeople are always looking at problems and challenges with a view to solving them instead of complaining about them or blaming others. They aim at solving problems rather than placing blame.

**Commitment.** Successful people are willing to make personal sacrifices through long hours and loss of leisure time. They are unfailingly committed and reliable to whatever they are doing. They can be counted on to get the job done and always make a positive contribution.

**Patience.** A very interesting quality of successful businesspeople, irrespective of their swiftness in judgment and decision making, is that they tend to know when to wait and vice versa. Patience and commitment go hand in hand, and the patient businesspeople who dedicate themselves to working away at their business day after day reap the rewards of their patience.

**Realistic expectations.** Ralph Marston once said, *"Don't lower your expectations to meet your performance. Raise your level of performance to meet your expectations."* However, to be successful, you will have to keep your expectations realistic. It is one of the best ways to keep from getting frustrated when things don't happen as quickly as you'd like them to.

**Risk.** Another quality of successful people is their relentless desire for risk. Treading where no one has treaded before and taking up challenges others would run away from or simply complain at.

**Perseverance.** The ability to continue despite setbacks, financial insecurity, and exposure to risk is necessary. Successful people move toward the pictures they create in their minds. They can rehearse coming actions or events as they "see" them and persevere until that picture becomes real.

**Personal and professional integrity.** Having a keen sense of integrity is important to ensure that business transactions are conducted with ethics in mind. Don Galer said, *"Integrity is what we do, what we say, and what we say we do."* A successful businessperson conducts him or herself in a respectable manner and always acts fairly and responsibly. Richard Buckminster Fuller stated, *"Integrity is the essence of everything successful."* Those who ignored this principle later regretted it when all they built crumbled right before them after being found out.

**Driven by accomplishments, not money.** Successful businesspeople follow the theory of Apple Inc.'s founder, Steve Jobs, who said, *"The journey is the reward."* They are customer-focused, not product-focused.

**Negotiators.** You have to be good or develop the ability to negotiate skillfully to make it in business. Howard Baker explains that *"the most difficult thing in any negotiation, almost, is making sure that you strip it off the emotion and deal with the facts."* Almost every business transaction has to be negotiated to get it signed off. In the words of Chester Karrass, *"In business, you don't get what you deserve, you get what you negotiate for."*

**Time management.** Your ability to manage time is a key to being successful, not only in business but in life. Peter Drucker said, *"Time is the scarcest resource and unless it is managed nothing else can be managed."*

Succeeding in business is more than buying and selling products. All the above qualities as well as some that were not mentioned can go a long way to influence a businessperson's ability to manage a business of any size at any level and still succeed, ensuring growth and profitability.

# 9. BUSINESS SKILLS AND KNOWLEDGE TO DEVELOP

*"Success always comes when preparation meets opportunity."*

– Henry Hartman, *a commercial graphic designer,
illustrator and fine art painter and drawer*

There are also certain business skills that can enhance your understanding of how to successfully start and manage a business. To some extent, Mitch Thrower, a business entrepreneur and author, was quite right in saying, *"Implementers don't care about the origins of ideas or the creative process; they are too busy with their own concerns, while idea people often don't value the necessary financial and business management skills necessary for execution."*

However, for many new businesses, it is almost certain you will be both the originator of the idea and the implementer, at least in the initial stages. It is in your best interest to start by assessing your business knowledge and skills level. This will help you decide whether you need to learn new skills or draw on outside help by delegating, recruiting, or outsourcing aspects of the business not within your skill base to enable you focus on what you are more capable at. Having said that, developing these skills can help you better understand the business for effective and efficient management. Peter Drucker once made a distinction between efficient and effective business skills. He said, *"Performing an activity swiftly and economically is efficient, while doing the right thing well is effective."* Among the basic skills to focus on are:

**People management.** Develop the skill to manage people recruitment, resolve disputes, motivate staff, and manage training.

Good people management will help employees to work together as a well-functioning team.

**Product development.** You will need to make long-term plans for product development and identify the people, materials, and processes required to achieve them. Making such plans means understanding your competition and your customers' needs.

**Marketing skills.** Develop a sound marketing approach that will help you set up and oversee sales and marketing operations, analyze markets, identify selling points for your product, and follow these through to market your product or service.

**Sales skills.** Selling your product or service is the lifeline to a business. Without it, your business cannot survive or grow. You need to be able to identify potential customers and their individual needs, explain your goods and services effectively to them, and convert these potential customers into clients. Be conscious of the fact that *"there is only one boss, the customer. And he can fire everybody in the company from the chairman on down, simply by spending his money somewhere else"* (Sam Walton).

**Supplier relationship management.** If you work with suppliers, you will have to identify suppliers and positively manage your relationships with them.

**Financial management.** This includes having a good understanding of cash flow planning and credit management and maintaining good relationships with your accountant and bank.

**Operations.** This involves learning to be able to coordinate various aspects of the day-to-day inner workings of the business to achieve the highest possible output and finding ways and strategies that can respond effectively to changing environments and needs of customers.

**Strategic Management.** In simple terms, strategic management involves analyzing the business, deciding how to address issues that come up in the analysis, and taking the needed actions in order to create and sustain the business's competitive advantage. It also involves defining what the business objectives are for the entire organization and each unit and how best to achieve these objectives with what resources.

In conclusion, as Brian Tracy said, *"Your earning ability today is largely dependent upon your knowledge, skill and your ability to combine that knowledge and skill in such a way that you contribute value for which customers are going to pay."* To effectively manage a new business or, for that matter, an existing business, it is essential to have a fair understanding of these skills to be able to develop the right balance for sustainable growth in sales and profitability.

# 10. How to Put a
# Compelling Plan Together

*"Before everything else, getting ready is the secret of success."*

– Henry Ford, *a prominent American industrialist and
founder of the Ford Motor Company*

My experience in the field has exposed to me the level of confusion many associate with the subject of business planning. I find people who are honestly so intimidated with writing a business plan that they have never started the business they dreamt of. Others question its importance because they think it's only for securing external funding, and because they are not interested in any external funding they decide there is no need to consider putting one together. There are countless others who just never bothered about it. Some simply consulted their accountants or business advisors to write it for them. Unfortunately, for some of this last group of people, their presentations to bankers and investors were not convincing enough to secure the needed funding.

As a principle, I only provide this service for my clients if they agree for us to do it together, especially if it is for the purposes of securing funding. That way, they get to be involved and are in the position to explain the underlying assumptions behind the content.

An international consultant, Dr. Graeme Edwards, once said, *"It's not the plan that is important, it's the planning."* The real value of creating the business plan is not in having the finished product in hand; rather, the value lies in the process of researching and thinking about your business in a systematic way. The act of planning helps you to think things through thoroughly, study and research if you are not sure of the facts, and look at your ideas critically. A business plan is a futuristic document, and almost every point in there is based on one assumption or the other.

A business plan is simply putting together a written document that describes a business, its objectives, its strategies, the market it's in, and its financial forecasts. The process of writing a good business plan, among other things, will help put together your ideas and research into a more structured format, clarify the purpose of the business, verify that the business idea is realistic and commercially viable, essentially help set sales and financial targets, plan for the future of the business, and set out the business and marketing strategies.

It has both internal and external uses. For internal purposes, it can be used to help measure success, focus on development efforts, help spot potential pitfalls before they manifest, and structure the financial aspects of a business. On the other hand, it is used externally to introduce the business to or apply for funding from bankers, external investors (friends, venture capitalist firms), grant providers, potential buyers of the business, and potential partners.

Whichever way you look at it, the business plan is simply one of the most essential pieces of documentation that any person starting a business needs to consider putting together. In the words of Chris Corrigan, an Australian businessman, *"You can't overestimate the need to plan and prepare. In most of the mistakes I've made, there has been this common theme of inadequate planning beforehand. You really can't over-prepare in business!"*

Planning is key in ensuring the continuous existence of an existing business. Every business that seeks to be successful must regularly review its business plan to ensure it continues to meet its needs. It is sensible to review current performance on a regular basis and identify the most likely strategies for growth. Once you have reviewed your progress and identified the key growth areas that you want to target, it's time to revisit your business plan and make it a road map to the next stages of your business.

For a new business, it is important to establish the purpose of the plan from the onset, because the emphasis of any plan should be dependent on the intended user. In the next few pages, I am going to discuss the essential components of a typical business plan. This guide, when used with my uniquely designed template *(you can contact me to order your template)*, can help you write a compelling business plan. It will save you a lot of consultation hours. For most of my clients, I offer the template and guide, encouraging them to complete the template and bring it over for us to professionally fine-tune together for the intended purpose. A typical plan includes:

## An Executive Summary

The executive summary is an overview of the business you want to start, a synopsis of the key points of your entire plan. It should include highlights from each section of the rest of the document, from the key features of the business opportunity to the elements of the financial forecasts. It should clearly and concisely address each of the following subjects:

- Overview of the company
- Recap of the opportunity. Quantify and describe the opportunity and where you fit. Explain why you are in business along with the reasons you will be able to take advantage of this opportunity.
- Brief summary of the market. How large is the market and stage of development (early growth versus mature). What are the key drivers, trends, and influences in the market?
- Differentiation. What separates you from the rest of the pack? Is your product proprietary, patented, copyrighted? Is your service or product better, faster, cheaper and, if so,

why? Is your advantage a temporary opportunity, and are there steps you can take to protect your position?

- Description of products or services. A very brief overview and description of your products and services.
- Management composition. It is said that investors invest in people not products. It's a proven fact that a company's management team is one of the best predictors of success, and investors will look very closely at the individuals who will be managing the company. The ideal scenario is that senior managers have previously started and successfully managed companies in the same business. Short of this, you want to emphasize the previous relevant experience of the management team. Names of companies and positions held and milestones achieved are worth emphasizing.
- Nature and use of proceeds. What type of funding are you looking for? Equity capital, grants, or loans? Under-capitalization is a major cause of new start-up business failure. You should have a very clear idea of how much money you will need to operate your business for the first full year (refer to *Appendix* for sample cost sheets). Banks loan officers and investors always want to know how the funds will be used.
- Key financials, such as, forecast cash flow statement and profit and loss account, etc.

The ultimate purpose of the executive summary is to explain the basics of your business in a way that both informs and interests the reader. If, after reading the executive summary, an investor or manager understands what the business is about and is keen to know more, it has done its job.

The executive summary should be concise, no longer than two pages at most, and interesting. For instance, if applying for a loan, state clearly how much you want, precisely how you are going to use it, and how the money will make your business more profitable, thereby ensuring repayment. It's advisable to write the executive summary of your plan after you've completed the rest.

## General Personal and Company Description

*Personal details*. Name, home address, telephone, mobile phone, date of birth, and marital status.

*Business details*. Business name, business address, telephone, fax, and e-mail.

*Mission statement*. Many companies have a brief mission statement, usually in thirty words or fewer, explaining their reasons for being and their guiding principles. If you want to draft a mission statement, this is a good place to put it in the plan.

*Company goals and objectives*. Goals are destinations. Objectives are progress markers along the way to goal achievement.

*Business philosophy*. What is important to you in business?

*To whom will you market your products?* State it briefly here—it should be dealt with more thorough in the *Marketing Plan* section.

*Describe your industry*. Is it a growth industry? What changes do you foresee in the industry, short-term and long-term? How will your company be poised to take advantage of them?

*Describe your most important company strengths and core competencies*. What factors will make the company succeed? What do you think your major competitive strengths will be? What background experience, skills, and strengths do you personally bring to this new venture?

*Legal form of ownership*. Sole proprietor, partnership, corporation, limited liability company or corporation? Why have you selected this form?

*Exit strategy.* You may want to explain to investors how they will get their money back, what you are anticipating they will recover in excess of their investment, and in what time frame.

Possible exit strategies can include the sale or merger of your company, a management buyout, an IPO, or a private placement.

## Products and Services

Describe in depth your products or services. Technical specifications, drawings, photos, sales brochures, and other bulky items belong in *Appendices*. Discuss pricing, service, support, warranty, production, etc.

What are the advantages of your products or services, and how do they compare to the competition? Examples include level of quality or unique or distinguishing features. What is the timetable for introducing these products, and what steps need to be taken to assure that this timeline is met? Are there other vendors involved, and if so, who, and where do they fit? Have your products been tested or evaluated, and if so, where, when, and what were the results? Are there plans for future or next-generation products, and if so, what and when? Are these new products included in your revenue and cost projections?

## Marketing Plan

### RESEARCH

**Why?** It is quite deceptive to assume that you already know about your intended market. You need to do market research to make sure you are on track. Use the opportunity to uncover data and to question your marketing efforts.

**How?** There are two kinds of market research: primary and secondary.

**Primary research** means gathering your own data.

**Secondary research** means using published information, such as industry profiles, trade journals, newspapers, magazines, census data, and demographic profiles. This type of information is available in public libraries, industry associations, chambers of commerce, from vendors who sell to your industry, and from government agencies.

In your marketing plan, be as specific as possible: give statistics, numbers, and sources. The marketing plan will be the basis later on of all important sales projections.

### Facts about your industry:
- What is the total size of your market?
- What percentage share of the market will you have?
- Current demand in target market
- Trends in target market—growth trends, trends in consumer preferences, and trends in product development
- Growth potential and opportunity for a business of your size

### What barriers to entry do you face in entering this market with your new company? Some typical barriers may include:
- High capital costs
- High production costs
- High marketing costs
- Consumer acceptance and brand recognition
- Training and skills
- Unique technology and patents
- Unions
- Shipping costs
- Tariff barriers and quotas

### How will you overcome the barriers? How could the following affect your company?
- Change in technology
- Change in government regulations
- Change in the economy
- Change in your industry

## PRODUCTS

In the *Products and Services* section, you described your products and services as you see them. Now, describe them from your customers' points of view.

*Features and benefits.* List all of your major products or services.

For each product or service:

- Describe the most important features. What is special about it?
- Describe the benefits. That is, what will the product do for the customer?

Note the difference between features and benefits, and think about them. For example, a house that gives shelter and lasts a long time is made with certain materials and to a certain design; those are its features. Its benefits include pride of ownership, financial security, providing for the family, and inclusion in a neighborhood. You build features into your product so that you can sell the benefits.

What after-sale services will you give? Some examples are delivery, warranty, service contracts, support, follow-up, and refunds.

## CUSTOMERS

Identify your targeted customers, their characteristics, and their geographic locations, i.e., their demographics. The description will be completely different depending on whether you plan to sell to other businesses or directly to consumers. Then, for each customer group, construct what is called a demographic profile, including age, gender, location, income level, social class, occupation, and education level. For business customers, the demographic factors might be industry, location, size of firm, quality, technology, and price preferences.

## COMPETITION

What products and companies will compete with you? List your major competitors (names and addresses). Will they compete with you across the board, or just for certain products, certain customers, or in certain locations?

Will you have important indirect competitors? For example, video rental stores compete with theaters, although they are different types of businesses. How will your products or services compare with the competition?

Other areas to consider: niche, marketing strategy, promotion, promotional budget, pricing (explain your methods of setting prices), proposed location, and distribution channels (how you sell your products or services: retail, direct (mail order, web, catalog), wholesale, your own sales force, agents, independent representatives, bid on contracts).

## SALES FORECAST

It's time to attach some numbers to your plan. Use a sales forecast spreadsheet to prepare a month-by-month projection. Forecast should be based on your historical sales, the marketing strategies that you have just described in your market research, and industry data, if available.

You may want to do two forecasts:

1) A "best guess," which is what you really expect.
2) A "worst case" low estimate that you are confident you can reach no matter what happens.

Remember to keep notes on your research and your assumptions as you build this sales forecast and all subsequent spreadsheets in the plan. This is critical if you are going to present it to funding sources.

## SWOT ANALYSIS

A SWOT analysis simply helps you to assess your *Strengths* and *Weaknesses*, and the *Opportunities* and *Threats* your business faces or may face in the course of operations. It provides a clear basis for examining your business performance and prospects.

There are various ways by which you can assess your *Strengths*. Continual dialogue with customers or potential customers and suppliers may also provide a clue as to where your strengths are. Rising sales, for an existing business, in a particular product, a strong balance sheet, positive cash flow, growing turnover and profitability, skilled financial management, skilled employees, successful recruitment, effective training and development, modern, low-cost production facilities, a good location, market leadership in a profitable niche, an established customer base, a strong product range, effective research and development, a skilled sales team, and thorough after-sales service, are all good indicators.

*Weaknesses*, on the other hand, can be known through various indicators, most of which are the opposite of the strength of the business. They are usually known but tend to be ignored. Not having the right financial management expert or system in place will result in poor credit control, leading to unpredictable cash flow or insufficient funds unavailable for investment. Others may be a limited or outdated product range, complacency and failure to innovate, over-reliance on few customers, expertise and control locked up in a few key personnel, high staff turnover, long leases tying the business to unsuitable premises or equipment, inefficient processes, outdated equipment, high cost of production, and low productivity.

Changes in the business's external environment can provide great *Opportunities*, which, when well managed, can be turned into an advantage for the business. External factors include things such as improved access to potential new customers and markets overseas, the development of new distribution channels such as the Internet, deterioration in a competitor's performance or the insolvency of a competitor, securing financiers to fund expansion, which could be as a result of political, legislative, or regulatory change, economic trends such as a fall in interest rates, introduction of new technology for a process, increased sales to existing customers or new leads gained through them, and social developments such as demographic changes.

*Threats* can be major or minor. Minor threats can equally affect your business and have far-reaching consequences on the business, destroying its survival and profitability. It can be in the form of loss of a significant customer, price rises from suppliers, lenders reducing credit lines or increasing charges, improved competitive products or the emergence of new competitors, key personnel leaving, perhaps with trade secrets, new technology that makes your products obsolete or gives competitors an advantage, legal action taken against you by a customer, social developments such as consumer demands for environmentally friendly or ethics-based products, political, legislative, and regulatory changes such as new regulations increasing your costs or requiring product redesign.

The results of SWOT analyses should not be the end but rather a starting point. You can capitalize on the results and play to your strengths, as each business is different. Opportunities that are in line with your strengths may prompt you to pursue a strategy of aggressive expansion.

You should prioritize the weaknesses and address those that can be addressed. Weaknesses that cannot be addressed now must be acknowledged and respected until time and resources allow a solution. Some weaknesses can be turned into strengths or opportunities, such as turning a shortage of production capacity into scarcity value for your product. Other weaknesses, such as financial ones, might be solved by raising further funds, or management shortcomings solved by recruiting new personnel. Some will need a significant investment in time and resources over time. You may for instance, need to start a program of improvements through training or quality management. The analysis could also suggest other strategic options for the business, such as taking defensive measures in areas of threat where weakness had been identified or diversifying away from areas of significant threat to more promising opportunities.

Some of the ways of protecting your business against the threats include fostering good employee relations, taking out insurance cover against obvious potential disasters, investing in legal protection for your intellectual property, taking advantage of low fixed interest rates to move your overdraft to long-term loans, ensuring you have clear and reasonable contracts with suppliers, customers, and employees, building relationships with suppliers and customers, drawing up realistic contingency plans to cope with potential crises, and introducing the right types of service contracts for key personnel.

## Operational Plan

Explain the daily operation of the business, its location, equipment, people, processes, and surrounding environment.

*Production.* How and where are your products or services produced?

*Location.* What qualities do you need in a location? Describe the type of location you'll have.

*Legal environment.* Licensing and bonding requirements, permits, health, workplace, or environmental regulations, special regulations covering your industry or profession, etc.

*Personnel.* Number of employees, type of labor, where you find the right employees. Quality of existing staff, pay structure, training methods and requirements, task breakdown, etc.

*Inventory.* What kind of inventory will you keep: raw materials, supplies, finished goods? Average value in stock (i.e., what is your inventory investment). Rate of turnover and how this compares to the industry averages. Seasonal buildups. Lead time for ordering.

*Suppliers.* Identify key suppliers, with names and addresses, type and amount of inventory furnished, credit and delivery policies, history, and reliability.

*Credit policies.* Do you plan to sell on credit? Do you really need to sell on credit? Is it customary in your industry and expected by your clientele? If yes, what policies will you have about who gets credit and how much? How will you check the creditworthiness of new applicants? What terms will you offer your customer—that is, how much credit, and when will payment be due?

*Managing your accounts receivable.* If you do extend credit, you should do an aging (aging report is a list of customers' accounts receivable amounts by how long they are owed. It alerts management to any slow paying customers) at least monthly to track how much of your money is tied up in credit given to customers and to alert you to slow payment problems.

*Managing your accounts payable.* You should also age your accounts payable, what you owe to your suppliers. This helps you plan whom to pay and when. Paying too early depletes your cash, but paying late can cost you valuable discounts and can damage your credit.

## Management and Organization Plan

Who will manage the business on a day-to-day basis? What experience does that person bring to the business? What special or distinctive competencies does he or she have? Is there a plan for continuation of the business if this person is lost or incapacitated?

The section should go into some detail about the individuals who will be entrusted with the investor's money. Stress relevant experience and previous success. This section of the plan should include:

- Biographic summary of key management
- Organizational charts (current and future)
- Manpower table
- Board of advisors
- Board of directors

If you'll have more than ten employees, create an organizational chart showing the management hierarchy and who is responsible for key functions. Include position descriptions for key employees. If you are seeking loans or investors, include resumes (in the *Appendices*) of owners and key employees.

### Professional and Advisory Support
List the following:
- Board of directors
- Management advisory board
- Attorney
- Accountant
- Insurance agent

### Personal Financial Statement
Include personal financial statements for each owner and major stockholder, showing assets and liabilities held outside the business and personal net worth. Owners will often have to draw on personal assets to finance the business, and these statements will show what is available. Bankers and investors usually want this information as well.

It is also important that thought goes into the amount of money that you require per month to maintain your current standard of living, let alone improve it. The business needs to know how much you require so that pricing decisions can be realistically made.

### Start-Up Expenses and Capitalization
You will have quite a number of expenses before you even begin operating your business. It's important to estimate these expenses accurately and then to plan where you will get sufficient capital. Remember, this will include the money for buying or leasing premises, making those premises suitable for your business (even if working from home, you may need to convert a room into an office), any equipment you may need, and working money to get

you through those first lean months as the business becomes established.

Some of the quick questions that need to be realistically answered are: Where will I get the money that I need to start up my business? Do I have money of my own? Can my family and friends help me? Do I qualify for an existing government grant or scheme? Is a loan from the bank my best option? How much will the interest rate be?

The more thorough your research efforts, the less chance that you will leave out important expenses or underestimate them. A rule of thumb is that contingencies should equal at least 20 percent of the total of all other start-up expenses.

Explain your research and how you arrived at your forecasts of expenses. Give sources, amounts, and terms of proposed loans. Also explain in detail how much will be contributed by each investor and what percent ownership each will have. Sample Set Up Cost page can be found as Appendix I.

## Financial Plan

The financial plan may consist of twelve months' or one to five years' profit and loss projection, a cash-flow projection, a projected balance sheet, and a break-even calculation. Together, they constitute a reasonable estimate of your company's financial future. More importantly, the process of thinking through the financial plan will improve your insight into the inner financial workings of your company.

*Projected cash flow.* If the profit projection is the heart of your business plan, cash flow is the blood. Businesses fail because they cannot pay their bills. Every part of your business plan is important, but none of it means a thing if you run out of cash. Sample forecast Cash Flow Statement can be found as Appendix II.

*Profit and loss statement.* The primary tool for good financial reporting is the profit and loss statement. This is a measure of a company's sales and expenses over a specific period of time. It is prepared at regular intervals (monthly for the first year and annually through five years) to show the results of operating during those accounting periods. It should follow generally accepted accounting principles and must contain specific revenue and expense categories regardless of the nature of the business. Sample forecast Profit and Loss Statement can be found as Appendix III.

**Opening day balance sheet.** A balance sheet is one of the fundamental financial reports that any business needs for reporting and financial management. A balance sheet shows what items of value are held by the company (assets) and what its debts are (liabilities). When liabilities are subtracted from assets, the remainder is owners' equity. Sample forecast Balance Sheet Statement can be found as Appendix IV.

**Break-even analysis.** A break-even analysis predicts the sales volume, at a given price, required to recover total costs. The sales level is the dividing line between operating at a loss and operating at a profit. Expressed as a formula, break-even is:

$$\text{Breakeven Sales} = \frac{\text{Fixed Costs}}{1 - \text{Variable Costs}}$$

where fixed costs are expressed in dollars, but variable costs are expressed as a percent of total sales.

Everything you've included in the plan up to this point should support your financial assumptions and projections. In other words, the reader shouldn't be surprised when they see your three- to five-year revenue forecast because you've given them detailed information on the market, the opportunity, and your strategies. You've described the advantages that you have over competition; you have outlined how you plan to reach the market and the management team that you have to help you achieve your objectives. Your projections should represent a logical conclusion to everything that you've included in the plan.

Finally, *as Ronald Reagan said, "Each generation goes further than the generation preceding it because it stands on the shoulders of that* generation. You will have opportunities beyond anything we have ever known." Francis Bacon, Sr, said, *"The wise man will make more opportunities than he finds."* And, in the words of Robert Schuller, *"High achievers spot rich opportunities swiftly, make big decisions quickly and move into action immediately. Follow these principles and you can make your dreams come true."*

## Appendices
Include details and studies in your business plan. For example, include:
- Brochures and advertising materials
- Industry reports and information
- Forecasted profit and loss statement
- Forecasted cash flow statement
- Blueprints and plans, maps and photos of location
- Magazine articles or other articles
- Detailed lists of equipment owned or to be purchased
- Copies of leases and contracts
- Letters of support from future customers
- Any other materials needed to support the assumptions in this plan,
- Market research studies
- List of assets available as collateral for a loan

### Fine-Tuning The Plan For An Intended User
The generic business plan presented above should be modified to suit your specific type of business and the audience for which the plan is written.

### *For Raising Capital*
***For bankers***. Bankers want assurance of orderly repayment. If you intend using this plan to present to lenders, include:
- The amount of loan and how the funds will be used, what the funds will accomplish and how they will make the business stronger

- Requested repayment terms (number of years to repay). You will probably not have much negotiating room on interest rate but may be able to negotiate a longer repayment term, which will help cash flow.
- Collateral offered, and a list of all existing liens against collateral

**For investors.** Investors have a different perspective. They are looking for dramatic growth, and they expect to share in the rewards. Include information about:
- Funds needed short-term
- Funds needed in two to five years
- How the company will use the funds, and what this will accomplish for growth
- Estimated return on investment
- Exit strategy for investors (buyback, sale, or IPO)
- Percent of ownership that you will give up to investors
- Milestones or conditions that you will accept
- Financial reporting to be provided
- Involvement of investors on the board or in management

As comprehensive as this guide may be, the time and resources you invest in putting it together is very important for achieving the right result. Whether it is for internal or external use, you owe it to yourself to establish the underlying assumptions that are realistic and consistent with the industry of your choice.

*"You are the embodiment of the information you choose to accept and act upon. To change your circumstances you need to change your thinking and subsequent actions"* (Adlin Sinclair).

# 11. CONCLUSION

*"When written in Chinese, the word 'crisis' is composed of two characters—one represents danger and the other represents opportunity."*

– John F. Kennedy, *35th President of the United States*

In conclusion, in the midst of the economic downturn, there are many who have found the way to lift their heads above the storms. Most of these people, I believe, may not have necessarily planned to do so. However, the challenges of the times and life have a very interesting way of squeezing out the creativity in us, if not for anything at all, for the survival instinct in man. Jonathan Schattke said, *"Necessity is the mother of invention, it is true, but its father is creativity, and knowledge is the midwife."* And at times, as Brian Koslow said, *"the freedom to move forward to new opportunities and to produce results comes from living in the present not the past."*

The times we are in are undoubtedly some of the best times, that is, only if you decide to look at it the other way around. Many have taken advantage of the opportunities staring right up in their faces. Fresh millionaires are being made each day. At the same time, businesses are closing their doors and others are giving up, while their competitors are seizing the opportunities.

The ability to cease opportunities by connecting problems and questions with solutions and answers and turning them into viable money-making business ventures is one of the most creative things any individual can do to transform his or her life. Mary Lou Cook, an American educationist, once said, *"Creativity is inventing, experimenting, growing, taking risks, breaking rules, making mistakes, and having fun."*

Interestingly, opportunities do not often show up with labels and signposts. The big ones we tend to wish for and daydream about seldom come by, and if any turn up, chances of accessing them and owning them are very slim. Experienced surfers will tell you that waiting for the big wave can take a very long while, and when it comes, you might only have one shot at it because even *"ability is of little account without opportunity"* (Napoleon). Jumping at several smaller opportunities daily has proven over time to be the better prospect. If you ignore a chance, someone else will surely find it.

Unfortunately, they will be the ones to enjoy the fruits should the idea succeed. Being creative as you go about your daily activities and engaging your brain can help you solve almost every problem there is in life. And you will be glad to know that life only pays you for the problems you solve. Woody Allen, an American screenwriter, director, and author, sums it up this way, *"Summing up, it is clear the future holds great opportunities. It also holds pitfalls. The trick will be to avoid the pitfalls, seize the opportunities, and get back home by six o'clock."*

To have an upper hand over the economic downturn as you start and grow your business:

- Set specific objectives and plan your days around what you need to get done to generate income.
- Learn to focus on what you are best at to make your products and services better and let others handle aspects you are least capable of handling. Adding value to your products and services tends to be far more appealing to customers than just lowering prices.
- Stick to the line of business you are passionate about and more able to survive the times with. That is, if you have other lines of business, expand existing lines that are doing well. Look at the competition, rename, repack-

age, and re-price your products, offering multiple price options to the customer. Customers will more likely choose among the options you are offering instead of looking for alternative sellers.

- Better still, develop products and services that address the current market needs and are able to generate the quickest income. Or develop a niche product for a segment of your market that is more resilient in the face of the changes in the economy. Or identify a new market, plan, and access it.

- Ensure that you have enough capital from the onset. Like they say, "cash is king." Lower cash flow can potentially suck the life out of the business. Make every effort to search for and take advantage of trade offers and discounts to free up cash. Even if you have to borrow, revisit your assumptions in line with current economic conditions. Otherwise, work at decreasing expenditure (such as taking advantage of webinars to cut down travel cost) and increase cash revenue (less selling on credit) with the aim to increase profits with time.

- Review your business and marketing plan and make the needed changes to reflect the direction of the market with an eye on the marketing expenses. In effect, adapt new strategies to address the changes. You may, for instance, re-evaluate your pricing strategy and decide to offer discounts on your most popular products and services.

- If there is any time to give more attention to existing and past customers, it is now. Reach out more to them, reminding them of your continued business with them. Make available to them cash rewards and gift incentives for referrals from them.

- It is also a great time to evaluate your procedures and operational policies and make improvements to make it relevant to the current market conditions and customer needs. Use customer surveys and feedback, and ask basic questions such as: Are customer services teams providing the best service? Do the sales teams need new training? Are there any, and what, better ways to improve performance and growth?

- A time of laxity in business is a great opportunity to expand your knowledge base by taking up new courses, reading new books, networking with others in the industry, getting involved in trade associations, and even seeking joint venture and partnerships.

- Do everything to study and understand the market on how your products and services are affected by the changes in the economy and build on your competitive advantage.

To start and grow a business to survive the economic downturn is a sure recipe for succeeding in the good economic times. That is exactly what this book offers you: an opportunity to look at the economic downturn differently and take advantage of the great opportunities it presents as you seek to earn income or extra income or to fulfill a dream.

## Step-by-Step Checklist

Here's a quick rundown of the basic steps to a great start in starting and growing a business.

1.  Have a clear idea of:
    a.  Product or service. What your USP (Unique Selling Point) will be. Be **passionate** about it.
    b.  Branding. Choose a name, logo, and slogan consistent with your aim and target audience. Ensure quality designs of letterhead, business cards, etc.
    c.  Your target group.
    d.  Market research.
2.  Develop the idea with the customer in mind, as well as yourself and your ability to compete.

3. Decide the business model. Office, home-based, licensing, multi-level marketing, drop shipping?

4. Decide on where to start from: part time or full time?

5. Decide how you will produce the product or supply the service.

6. Check out any regulations and licenses involved.

7. Decide how much to charge for your product or service.

8. Decide how to market and sell your product or service: direct mail, telemarketing, designing and printing (flyers, brochures, etc.), exhibitions, websites, research, surveys, promotions, press releases, public relations, photography, and advertising.

9. Decide the legal structure (sole trader, partnership, limited liability company, etc.) that will favor you. Register the business where necessary. Resolve who will manage the business.

10. Decide on your capital requirements and how to fund it. It will be in your interest to prepare a cash flow and profit and loss forecast for twelve months or one to five years, or both.

11. Get to know basic information about taxes, National Insurance, salaries and wages, and business rates.

12. Do everything possible to put your business plan together, either as a formal document or in any informal way you choose to write it.

Thank you for buying this book, and I hope you have or are about to take the necessary steps to start out. If you want to be like those who have stayed above the economic storms, then follow the steps I have laid out in this book to stay atop. According to Geri Weitzman, an American author and psychologist, "*Sometimes you gotta create what you want to be a part of.*" Go for it, and you will succeed one way or the other.

### End of My Writing, Starting Point for Your Action

# APPENDIX I

## Set up costs

| Setting Up the Business | £ |
|---|---|
| Business Consultancy/Advisory Services Fees | |
| Business Registration | |
| Business Logo, Letterhead, Business Cards | |
| Domain Name Registration & Website Design | |
| Licences | |
| Solicitor's Fees | |
| Insurance Premiums | |
| Workers Compensation | |
| | |
| **Setting Up the Premises** | |
| Lease Deposit and Advance Rent | |
| Business Rates | |
| Fittings & Refurbishment | |
| Utility - Water, Light, Heating | |
| Stationery and Office Supplies | |
| | |
| **Plant and Equipment** | |
| Equipment | |
| Vehicles | |
| Telecommunications | |
| Computers and Software | |
| | |
| **Starting Operations** | |
| Advertising and Promotion | |
| Raw Materials and Supplies | |
| Working Capital | |
| | |
| **Start-Up Capital** | |
| Equity Investment | |
| Borrowings | |
| Total | |
| | |
| **The result** | |
| Total Set-Up Costs | |
| Surplus Funds | |
| Borrowings Required | |

## APPENDIX II

| | Pre-Startup | Month 1 | Month 2 | Month 3 | Month 4 | Month 5 | Month 6 | Month 7 | Month 8 | Month 9 | Month 10 | Month 11 | Month 12 | Total |
|---|---|---|---|---|---|---|---|---|---|---|---|---|---|---|
| | £ | £ | £ | £ | £ | £ | £ | £ | £ | £ | £ | £ | £ | £ |
| **Receipts** | | | | | | | | | | | | | | |
| Owners' Capital | 0 | | | | | | | | | | | | | |
| Bank Loan / Cash Injection | | 0 | | | | | | | | | | | | 0 |
| Sales | | 0 | | | | | | | | | | | | 0 |
| Government Grant | | 0 | | | | | | | | | | | | 0 |
| **Total Cash Rcpts** | 0 | 0 | 0 | 0 | 0 | 0 | 0 | 0 | 0 | 0 | 0 | 0 | 0 | 0 |
| | | | | | | | | | | | | | | |
| **OVERHEADS** | | | | | | | | | | | | | | |
| Purchases | | 0 | 0 | 0 | 0 | 0 | 0 | 0 | 0 | 0 | 0 | 0 | 0 | 0 |
| Salaries | | 0 | 0 | 0 | 0 | 0 | 0 | 0 | 0 | 0 | 0 | 0 | 0 | 0 |
| Emp National Insurance | | 0 | 0 | 0 | 0 | 0 | 0 | 0 | 0 | 0 | 0 | 0 | 0 | 0 |
| Office Expenses | | 0 | 0 | 0 | 0 | 0 | 0 | 0 | 0 | 0 | 0 | 0 | 0 | 0 |
| Rent | | 0 | 0 | 0 | 0 | 0 | 0 | 0 | 0 | 0 | 0 | 0 | 0 | 0 |
| Telephone | | 0 | 0 | 0 | 0 | 0 | 0 | 0 | 0 | 0 | 0 | 0 | 0 | 0 |
| Business Rate | | 0 | 0 | 0 | 0 | 0 | 0 | 0 | 0 | 0 | 0 | 0 | 0 | 0 |
| Water Rates | | 0 | 0 | 0 | 0 | 0 | 0 | 0 | 0 | 0 | 0 | 0 | 0 | 0 |
| Subscription | | 0 | 0 | 0 | 0 | 0 | 0 | 0 | 0 | 0 | 0 | 0 | 0 | 0 |
| Bank Charges & Interest | | 0 | 0 | 0 | 0 | 0 | 0 | 0 | 0 | 0 | 0 | 0 | 0 | 0 |
| General Expenses | | 0 | 0 | 0 | 0 | 0 | 0 | 0 | 0 | 0 | 0 | 0 | 0 | 0 |
| Training & Development | | 0 | 0 | 0 | 0 | 0 | 0 | 0 | 0 | 0 | 0 | 0 | 0 | 0 |
| Heating & Lighting | | 0 | 0 | 0 | 0 | 0 | 0 | 0 | 0 | 0 | 0 | 0 | 0 | 0 |
| Insurance | | 0 | 0 | 0 | 0 | 0 | 0 | 0 | 0 | 0 | 0 | 0 | 0 | 0 |
| Loan Repayment | | 0 | 0 | 0 | 0 | 0 | 0 | 0 | 0 | 0 | 0 | 0 | 0 | 0 |
| Marketing | | 0 | 0 | 0 | 0 | 0 | 0 | 0 | 0 | 0 | 0 | 0 | 0 | 0 |
| Advertising | | | | | | | | | | | | | | |
| Professional Fees | | 0 | 0 | 0 | 0 | 0 | 0 | 0 | 0 | 0 | 0 | 0 | 0 | 0 |
| Delivery Charges | | | | | | | | | | | | | | |
| Travel Expenses | | | | | | | | | | | | | | |
| Vehicle Running Cost | | 0 | 0 | 0 | 0 | 0 | 0 | 0 | 0 | 0 | 0 | 0 | 0 | 0 |
| General Maintenance | | 0 | 0 | 0 | 0 | 0 | 0 | 0 | 0 | 0 | 0 | 0 | 0 | 0 |
| Registration Fees | 0 | | | | | | | | | | | | | |
| Professional Fees | 0 | | | | | | | | | | | | | |
| Capital Equipment | 0 | | | | | | | | | | | | | |
| Fixtures & Fittings | 0 | | | | | | | | | | | | | |
| Stock | 0 | | | | | | | | | | | | | |
| Market Research | 0 | | | | | | | | | | | | | |
| Marketing | 0 | | | | | | | | | | | | | |
| Refurbishment | 0 | | | | | | | | | | | | | |
| **Total Overheads** | 0 | 0 | 0 | 0 | 0 | 0 | 0 | 0 | 0 | 0 | 0 | 0 | 0 | 0 |
| Monthly Cash flow | | 0 | 0 | 0 | 0 | 0 | 0 | 0 | 0 | 0 | 0 | 0 | 0 | 0 |
| | | | | | | | | | | | | | | |
| **Opening Bal** | 0 | 0 | 0 | 0 | 0 | 0 | 0 | 0 | 0 | 0 | 0 | 0 | 0 | |
| **Closing Bal** | 0 | 0 | 0 | 0 | 0 | 0 | 0 | 0 | 0 | 0 | 0 | 0 | 0 | |

| Appendix III | | | |
|---|---|---|---|
| **XYZ LTD. YEAR 1 PROJECTED PROFIT & LOSS ACCOUNT** | | | |
| | | | |
| **Sales** | £ | - | |
| Cost/Goods Sold (COGS) | | - | |
| **Gross Profit** | £ | - | |
| | | | |
| **Less Overheads** | | | |
| Salaries | | - | |
| Emp National Insurance | | - | |
| Office Expenses | | - | |
| Rent | | - | |
| Telephone | | - | |
| Business Rate | | | |
| Water Rate | | - | |
| Subscription | | - | |
| Bank Charges and Interest | | - | |
| General Expenses | | - | |
| Training & Development | | - | |
| Heat and Light | | - | |
| Insurance | | - | |
| Loan Repayment | | - | |
| Marketing | | - | |
| Advertising | | - | |
| Accounting and Legal Fees | | - | |
| Delivery Charges | | - | |
| Travel Expenses | | | |
| Vehicle Running Cost | | - | |
| General Repairs & Maintenance | | - | |
| Taxes | | - | |
| Depreciation Furniture / Equipment / Vehicle | | - | |
| Other Expense (specify) | | - | |
| | | | |
| | | 0 | |
| | | | |
| **Net Profit before Tax** | | 0 | |

| Appendix IV | |
|---|---|
| **Balance Sheet Forecast** | |
| As at December 20 | |
| **Assets** | |
| Current assets | £0 |
| Cash | |
| Petty cash | |
| Accounts receivable | |
| Stock | |
| Short-term investment | |
| Prepaid expenses | |
| Long-term investment | |
| | |
| Fixed assets | £0 |
| Land | |
| Buildings | |
| Improvements | |
| Equipment | |
| Furniture | |
| Motor vehicles | |
| | |
| **Total assets** | £0 |
| **Liabilities** | |
| Current liabilities | £0 |
| Accounts payable | |
| Interest payable | |
| Taxes payable | |
| Income tax | |
| Sales tax | |
| Payroll accrual | |
| | |
| Long-term liabilities | £0 |
| Borrowings | |
| | |
| **Total liabilities** | £0 |
| **Net assets** | £0 |
| **Owner's equity** | |
| Retained earnings | |
| Current year earnings | £0 |
| **Total equity (should equal net assets)** | £0 |